NEVERTHELESS, GOD

God's best to you,
Sarah Kohlbrecher

NEVERTHELESS, GOD

A Study of Israel's Judges

Sarah Kohlbrecher

Nevertheless, God

Copyright © 2010
Sarah Kohlbrecher

ALL RIGHTS RESERVED
No portion of this publication may be reproduced, stored in any electronic system, or transmitted in any form or by any means, electronic, mechanical, photocopy, recording, or otherwise, without written permission from the author. Brief quotations may be used in literary reviews.

Library of Congress Number: 2010933742
ISBN: 978-0-9844841-2-6

FOR INFORMATION CONTACT:
Sarah Kohlbrecher
960 Miller Street S.
Shakopee, MN 55379
(952-496-2706)

Printed in the United States by Morris Publishing®
3212 East Highway 30
Kearney, NE 68847
1-800-650-7888

Because there is no greater sense of worth than to love and to be loved in return, humanity yearns for such acceptance. God is love; Scripture states that fact. In all that God is, He is love. Love is of God. But, unlike the old adage that love is blind, God is not impaired by imperfection. He is neither sightless nor blindfolded. God's infinite mercy endures forever. Therefore, God chooses to see through eyes of mercy to help us in the struggles of life. This book is dedicated to my fellow travelers, who, on the narrow way of life, have learned and re-learned that the Lord Jesus will confirm His Word to the obedient. This writing is for those who enjoy the fruit of obedience to Isaiah 34:16, "Seek ye out of the book of the LORD, and read."

Acknowledgments

All things are accomplished with teamwork. None of us have existence without resources and input from others. We are the product of a mass inflow of contributions. Achievements for which we personally take credit do not belong to us exclusively. Without God, we are nothing. Without interaction with people, we stagnate and wither. My many family members, friends, and the readers of my work have contributed much to my writing efforts.

Carl Sledge has done a superb job of the covers for this series of books. Bethany Sledge has been a joy to work with in editing. Of course, my dear husband has endured my frequent cries for help with the computer. He has prayed with me, laughed with me, and even cried with me through it all.

Those who have read my writings and have passed along kind words of encouragement have ministered to my need to feel that I can share some worthwhile blessings from God.

Thank you,

Sarah Kohlbrecher

Contents

Introduction	11
Chapter 1:	
Othniel, Israel's First Judge	13
Chapter 2:	
Ehud, God's Second Nevertheless	29
Chapter 3:	
Shamgar, the Plowman Judge	35
Chapter 4:	
Deborah: a Mother, a Judge	37
Chapter 5:	
Gideon, Israel's Man of Valor	49
Chapter 6:	
Abimelech, the Usurping Judge	71
Chapter 7:	
Tola, the Red Worm Judge	
Jair, the Enlightened Judge	83
Chapter 8:	
Jephthah, the Banished Judge, Returned	87
Chapter 9:	
Ibzan, Elon, and Abdon: Three Ordinary Men Who Judged Israel	105
Chapter 10:	
Samson, the Weak Superman	107
Chapter 11:	
Jonathan, a Displaced Levite Judge	131

Chapter 12:
  An Anonymous Levite Judge 137
Chapter 13:
  Ruth, an Unlikely Mother of the
    Eternal Judge   149
Epilogue 165

Introduction

Joshua was dead! The simple fact had a profound effect on the newly founded state of Israel. The young nation had been molded by only two leaders, Moses and Joshua. Moses had died before Israel possessed her land west of Jordan River. Joshua had then effectively led Israel across the Jordan and had established Israel's people in their promised homeland. He instituted governmental order and divided the land into twelve territories listed as the tribes of Israel. Under his leadership much of the mapped land that God had promised to Israel was conquered. However, when Joshua died, much was left to be done to shape Israel into a stable country under a unique theocratic authority of one God, named I AM JEHOVAH. That characteristic made Israel an enemy to the pagan worshipers in whose land she dwelt and among all the nations of the world. That uniqueness alone made Israel a reckoning force among the peoples of the civilized world. There was and has never been a god like unto Israel's JEHOVAH.

Under an oak tree by the sanctuary of the LORD was a great stone. That stone was witness to a covenant Joshua had made with Israel. The stone, named Ed, had heard all the LORD had spoken to Israel. Joshua wrote

Nevertheless, God

those words in the book of the law of God, and Israel swore to serve the LORD. She vowed to put away strange gods and to turn toward the LORD God of Israel. Remembering that parting pledge at the rock Ed, Israel sought God for leadership and direction. Until those leaders trained by Joshua died, Israel followed the LORD. However, soon after their deaths, Israel strayed from her moorings and embraced paganism. She quickly suffered degradation and humiliation at the hands of her enemies. When Israel repented, God sent a deliverer. Those deliverers were called judges in the Bible. In this book, they are referred to as exceptional persons interjected into Israel's plights as "Nevertheless, God . . ." (Judges 2:16).

Chapter 1
Othniel, Israel's First Judge

Israel faced a national crisis after Joshua died. Adding sorrow to sorrow, Israel had also lost Eleazar, their spiritual leader. Void of their leaders, they inquired of God who should lead them in battle against the Canaanites, who held much of Israel's promised land remaining to be conquered. The reply was not an appointment of a single man but, the LORD answered, "Judah shall lead you into battle. I have delivered the land into his hand." So the tribe of Judah invited some of the warriors from the tribe of Simeon to join the conquest. The two tribes made a pact to help each other conquer their promised territories. Together they slew ten thousand Canaanites and Perizzites in Bezek, in the territorial boundaries of Judah near the Jordan River.

However, the king of the "Ites" fled from Bezek. Israel pursued him and caught him. They cut off his thumbs and big toes. King Adoni–bezek confessed, "Seventy kings, from whom I had cut off their thumbs and big toes, gathered to eat at my table. As I have done, so God has requited me." A subtle plea for his life was interwoven in the boast. Those seventy kings had been humiliated with a magnitude that King Adoni–bezek felt was sufficient for his punishment as well. He deemed that rendering a conquered king incapable of grasping a weapon or being able to feed himself easily or to walk with proper balance was enough punishment. Israel remembered her pledge not to bargain with nor to make treaties with any of the heathen of Canaan. The warriors took the mighty king of Bezek to Jerusalem, and there he died in the raid and capture of the city.

Judah had fought against Jerusalem and had taken it. The inhabitants were killed, and the city was burned. Judah left the charred ruins to fight the Canaanites in the mountain and in the south and in the valley. From there Judah conquered Hebron and slew its leaders. Next, Israel pitched battle against Kirjath–sepher, Caleb's promised mountain. Faithful Caleb remained the only person alive in Israel of the adults who had come out of Egypt eighty-five years before.

The torching of Jerusalem ignited a hornet's nest. The Canaanites swarmed from the mountains and valleys of the south, headquartered at Kirjath–sepher. Caleb, Joshua's dear friend, yearned to possess that mountain. He made a proposal, "To him that smites Kirjath–sepher I will give my daughter, Achsah, to wife." The challenge was readily accepted.

"Uncle Caleb, I, Othniel, will accept that offer." Othniel was a son of Caleb's younger brother, Kenaz. Othniel did conquer the city and renamed it Debir. For her wedding gift, Achsah asked Caleb for a farm plot. He gave the couple the field Achsah desired. However, there were no sufficient water rights to the property.

"Othniel, you should ask Father for the water supply to the property," Achsah informed her husband.

Othniel, Israel's First Judge

"Saddle the donkey and go to ask him yourself," he replied.

The woman wasted no time in doing so. She rode her donkey to see her father. "I need to add to my request for payment for risking my husband's neck," she told Caleb.

Caleb knew his daughter's request had to be urgent for her to have left her honeymoon to return to her girlhood home. "What will that be?" he asked.

"Father, give me a blessing, for you gave me a south land with no water supply. Please give me springs of water from which my farm can be watered. That would make my wedding gift complete."

"Sure, my daughter. There are the upper springs and also the springs below. You may claim them all. May your farm be bountifully fruitful." Achsah gave her father a hug and remounted the donkey. She happily returned to her bridegroom. With that introduction, Othniel entered the pages of Israel's history. However, before the need arose for him to become a judge, more land had to be taken from the Canaanites for Israel. Othniel had joined the army, and he never went AWOL.

In the plains of Jericho, Moses' father-in-law's family had set up camp. Hobab, Jethro's son, had traveled with Israel through the wilderness and across the Jordan River. This family of Kenites were loyal to Israel but did not completely evolve into one with her. When Judah began battle against the Canaanites, the Kenites moved into the wilderness of Judah and dwelt among that tribe, enjoying the safety and protection. Judah and

Nevertheless, God

Simeon left the Kenites and began a campaign against Hormah, Gaza, Askelon, and Ekron. The LORD drove out the enemies in the mountain. Then, battle weary and spiritually depleted, Israel failed. She forgot her God almighty. "The Canaanites who live in the valley have chariots of iron. No way can we win against such superior warriors with such war machines!" complained the warriors. So the tribe of Judah laid down their swords and quit the fight.

The tribe of Dan also had problems. Amorites blocked the tribe of Dan from entering the valley. Confined to the mountain, Dan was stalemated. Joseph, his brother, prevailed against the Amorites in mount Heres, Aijalon, Shaalbim, and the coast of the Amorites while Dan fretted between the parentheses of faithlessness and unbelief.

Caleb, of the tribe of Judah, stood as a beacon of faith in the midst of the trouble. As Moses had predicted, Caleb had taken his mountain at age eighty-five. He had expelled the three sons of the giant Anak from Hebron. Caleb moved his large family into Hebron and the surrounding fields and villages. His testimony proved the promises of God. Caleb had peace while others around stewed in unbelief and failure.

Meanwhile, the tribe of Benjamin remained ineffectual and had begun to be satisfied merely to coexist with the Jebusites, who had rebuilt and had repopulated Jerusalem, which Judah had conquered and burned earlier in the conquest of Canaan. That city became a strong fortress for the enemy for many years.

Othniel, Israel's First Judge

The house of Joseph planned to fight against Bethel. Bethel was the historical place where Jacob had built an altar to the LORD and had made vows to Him as he fled from his brother, Esau. During the five hundred years after Jacob's altar, the heathen had built a thriving city of Luz on the site. Since Jacob had given his son, Joseph, that land, the tribal descendants of Joseph determined to possess it. Spies went to Luz to check it out. "There is a fellow coming out of the city alone. Let's capture him and make him talk." The spies patiently waited for the man to walk into their trap. They pinned him down a prisoner. "Tell us the easiest way we can get into Luz. Where is the city most vulnerable?"

"I won't talk," the man spat.

"If you don't talk, we will kill you," threatened the spies.

"And if I do? Then what?" the frightened man offered.

"Then you will live."

"What will you do to my city?" he inquired.

"We are going to wipe out the inhabitants. We are moving our people in."

"If I tell you the information, you must promise to spare my family."

"It's a deal. We'll spare your family, but you must spill the information and then move your family out without uttering a word about us. We warn you to keep your mouth shut, or you will die."

"I'll do it," the man said. The spies released him, and he turned to face Luz. "Follow me, and I will show

Nevertheless, God

you the entrance to the city." The man was true to his oath. The spies waited until the man had his family safely relocated. Israel's warriors destroyed the populace of Luz and possessed the town. The betrayer settled among the Hittites, built a new city, and named it Luz.

Manasseh, Joseph's oldest son, had problems as well. That tribe could not defeat the Canaanites in Beth-shean and her towns, in Taanach's towns, or in Dor, Ibleam, or Megiddo and her towns. Manasseh was too weak and faithless to conquer her land.

Eventually the Canaanites were made to pay taxes and rent to Israel (Judges 1:28). Those heathen became a torment to Israel just as God foretold through Moses and Joshua.

Ephraim, Joseph's younger son, also declared weakness. That tribe could not drive out the Canaanites in Gezer. The domino effect of fruitless negativity spread to the tribes of Zebulun, Asher, Naphtali, and Dan. Even though most of the Canaanites were made to pay tribute to Israel, the heathen tribes remained a constant threat to Israel's security. Most of Israel had become content to collect taxes from their enemies, who possessed large territories of rich land that Israel should have occupied. Their ineffective passiveness made God upset. The Amorites had forced the tribe of Dan into the mountain and had retaken the fertile valleys that Dan had hoped to till and farm. Failure was never God's desire for Israel.

When Israel exited Egypt decades before, God had sent an angel to go before them (Exodus 23:20-25). "Behold, I send an Angel before thee, to keep thee in the

Othniel, Israel's First Judge

way, and to bring thee into the place which I have prepared. Beware of him, and obey his voice, provoke him not; for he will not pardon your transgressions: for my name is in him. But if thou shalt indeed obey his voice, and do all that I speak; then I will be an enemy unto thine enemies, and an adversary unto thine adversaries. For mine Angel shall go before thee, and bring thee in unto the Amorites, and the Hittites, and the Perizzites, and the Canaanites, and the Hivites, and the Jebusites: and I will cut them off. Thou shalt not bow down to their gods, nor serve them, nor do after their works: but thou shalt utterly overthrow them, and quite break down their images. And ye shall serve the LORD your God, and he shall bless thy bread, and thy water; and I will take sickness away from the midst of thee."

    That unnamed angel had remained posted on duty but largely was inactive. Why? The angel of the LORD had been stationed at Gilgal, the first camp Israel had occupied after crossing Jordan River. At Camp Gilgal Israel received instructions for obtaining success and for thriving in health and prosperity. At Gilgal, Israel had received instructions and maps for possessing tribal territories. There, Joshua had circumcised the males, rolling away the reproach of Egypt from Israel. Right away, Israel began a successful campaign to conquer Canaan. Then Joshua grew old and Israel grew weary. Negotiating treaties to avoid war and compromising true worship subtly stripped Israel of her nationalistic pride as one nation governed by the LORD JEHOVAH, the I AM. The angel of the LORD was angry and disappointed with his charge. The angel left Gilgal and met Israel at Bochim nearby (Judges 2:1-3).

"And the angel of the LORD came up from Gilgal to Bochim, and said, I made you to go up out of Egypt, and have brought you unto the land which I sware unto your fathers; and I said, I will never break my covenant with you. And ye shall make no league with the inhabitants of this land; ye shall throw down their altars: but ye have not obeyed my voice: why have ye done this? Wherefore I also said, I will not drive them out from before you; but they shall be as thorns in your sides, and their gods shall be a snare unto you."

Israel repented that day with much weeping, but soon after Joshua's death she forsook the LORD God of her fathers and began to worship other gods of the people round about her. She provoked the LORD to anger. A new generation of Israelites had been born who had not witnessed the miracles God had done for Israel in the wilderness or in crossing Jordan. That young, modernized, and innovative generation revoked the old laws and established a new government, demanding religious tolerance and inclusion. Israel embraced the religions of the Canaanites and immersed herself in the cultures and practices of the very people God had warned her against. Intermarriages decayed the moral fabric and polluted the bloodline which God had established to preserve truth. God was livid over Israel's idolatry and immorality.

The heathen tribes of Canaan were largely descendants of Nimrod, the father of idolatry. Baal was a heathen god popular among the descendants of Nimrod,

Othniel, Israel's First Judge

the great-grandson of Noah. Nimrod had concocted various religions, promoting himself as Baal and his wife and child as equal gods in a plurality of beings known as Baalim. The religion promoted human sacrifices and sexually deviant practices in worship (II Chronicles 21:6, 11; 28:2-3). First Kings 18:28 describes the manner of worship that was also practiced. The prophets on Mount Carmel cried aloud and cut themselves after their manner with knives and lancets till the blood gushed out upon them. Nimrod's wife became known as Ashtoreth. Israel bowed to her and offered sacrifices to her (Psalm 106:36-38). Ashtoreth demanded human sacrifices and the burning of live infants in the arms of her furnace, a hollow, iron statue (Deuteronomy 12:31).

Those heathenish practices so provoked God's anger that Scripture records His anger was hot (Judges 2:14-16). "And the anger of the LORD was hot against Israel, and he delivered them into the hands of spoilers that spoiled them, and he sold them into the hands of their enemies round about, so that they could not any longer stand before their enemies. Whithersoever they went out, the hand of the LORD was against them for evil, as the LORD had . . . sworn unto them: and they were greatly distressed. *Nevertheless the LORD* raised up judges, which delivered them out of the hand of those that spoiled them" (emphasis mine).

Nevertheless! What a magnificent word! When God stated, "Nevertheless," mercy and hope came into focus as a light in extreme darkness. *Nevertheless*, the LORD raised up judges who delivered Israel from those

Nevertheless, God

who spoiled them. Israel's forsaking God and turning to idolatry brought her into bondage both economically and politically. Her farms were raided. Her towns were plundered. Israel lay wasted by those she had tolerated or accepted as equals. Israel had embraced their differences. Their new, covert friends became their masters.

The sad notation is recorded in Judges 2:15-19: "Whithersoever they went out, the hand of the LORD was against them for evil, as the LORD had said, and as the LORD had sworn unto them: and they were greatly distressed. Nevertheless the Lord raised up judges, which delivered them. . . . The LORD was with the judge, and delivered them out of the hand of their enemies all the days of the judge: for it repented the LORD because of their groanings by reason of them that oppressed them and vexed them. . . . When the judge was dead, . . . they returned, and corrupted themselves more than their fathers, in following other gods to serve them, and to bow down unto them; they ceased not from their own doings, nor from their stubborn way."

God's mercy and hope were dashed against the hard, stony hearts so that God revoked the pledge to drive out the enemy before Israel (Judges 2:20-21). What a sad parting for the angel of the LORD!

The angel had remained on duty for many decades and had driven out Israel's enemies as she advanced across the land of Canaan. When Israel gave up the fight against the heathen and allowed rebellion to creep in, she dismantled her assault plan for victory. The lack of spiritual perception blinded her eyes to the real reason she

Othniel, Israel's First Judge

existed and could enjoy freedom.

Furthermore, God said, "Through the nations left in Canaan after Joshua died, I will prove Israel whether they will keep the way of the LORD to walk in my way as their fathers did, or not." God left Israel to stew in a hotbed of distress and oppression from ruthless enemies. He had been forsaken by a self-sufficient, arrogant Israel. Therefore, God withdrew His angel, the shield of defense and offense. Israel spiraled downward, plunging into serious trouble.

Peace treaties, negotiations, intermarriages, tolerance, acceptance, and all other compromises and concessions that Israel made with the enemy had failed. The heathen were not interested in coexistence. They were out to destroy Israel completely and to purge Canaan of all Israelites. In the generation when Israel had lived in peace and safety under the peace treaty plans, Israel had dissolved her military and closed her training camps. However, her enemies had not been so careless. While Israel sang songs of pacifistic peace and harmony, her enemies were mustering men and creating war strategies with Mesopotamia. Frolicking in her romance with Baalim and worshiping in the groves of idolatry, Israel had become blinded to her own vulnerability. Steel jaws of slavery pinioned Israel to King Chushan–rishathaim of Mesopotamia for eight years. Servitude jolted Israel out of complacency and spiritual degradation. At last God was remembered.

Prayer meetings of repentance and cries to God moved Him to send the first "Nevertheless." Othniel,

Caleb's son-in-law, had not bowed to Baal. He had memories of Uncle Caleb's telling campfire stories about God's miracles. He recalled the goose bumps of excitement he felt as Caleb said, "I saw miracles with my own eyes. I heard with my ears the voice of Almighty God and saw the belching fire and dark smoke on Sinai. I ate miracle bread from heaven. The LORD God of Israel is one LORD. He alone can do such mighty works! He brought Israel out of slavery in Egypt. He parted the Red Sea and dried it up for us to cross. He led us through the wilderness and provided for us water from a rock. These shoes I now wear are the ones I wore when I left Egypt. Neither my shoes nor my clothes ever wore out. Neither did the wardrobe of all Israel wear out. Our feet didn't swell, and we lacked for nothing that God didn't supply! God dried up Jordan River so that I marched across with the thousands of Israel on dry land. God preserved my strength so that at age eighty-five I was equal to that of a forty-year-old man. I fought right along with those stalwart men less than half my age."

    Othniel remembered experiencing some of those miracles, and although Uncle Caleb was gone, Othniel vowed to keep true to the LORD God of Israel. He shuddered to think of his family being taxed and uselessly serving a heathen king. His hard-earned farm with its goodly springs was jeopardized. So, when God called, Othniel heard. His ears and heart were yearning for that call for national revival. Hot, earnest tears of repentance opened the ark of God in heaven for the anointing of God to empower a Nevertheless deliverer.

Othniel, Israel's First Judge

With a fresh anointing upon him, Othniel mustered an army to challenge King Chushan–rishathaim. Faith had restored hope. Obedience restored empowerment. Israel went to battle with her oppressor. The Spirit of the LORD came upon Othniel and his army. Victory came. As Israel's first anointed judge, Othniel led Israel into a spiritual renewal. He purged Israel of idolatry, and for forty years Israel had rest in the LORD. The sad conclusion to those forty years was that Othniel died leaving no successor to continue the revival.

It is often said that Israel was cruel and that her LORD God was cruel to give orders to wipe out the entire population of the land of Canaan. However, the severe judgments of God are not pronounced upon the innocent. God punishes the wicked evildoers. In the study of the heathen worship of the descendants of Ham who occupied Canaan, the Bible states that the man Nimrod founded many of the influential hubs of culture and religion in and around Canaan, Nineveh, and Babylon. The gods that Nimrod introduced were icons and idols representing himself, his wife, and their son as a plurality of gods named Baalim. Individual names were given to the different idols representing Nimrod and his family, Baal, Ashtoreth, and others. A golden calf was a popular form in Egypt, the land of Ham's descendants, who also worshiped other creatures from the animal and insect realms representing nature in various forms of energy and life. Nimrod had been declared as the creator and giver of life and pleasure. In Canaan, metal statues were made as furnaces on which sacrifices could be laid and burned. This practice was common in the worship to both Baal and Ashtoreth. Ezekiel 16:1-40 describes the worship to these idols. This polluted concept of worship caused the LORD to pronounce the sentence of death upon the practitioners. Ezekiel related the horrible worship style. Israel had taken the wealth that the LORD had given to her and made images of men of them, images which she worshiped. Israel had built dedicated places to idols in every street. She had built an eminent place known today as a brothel for the worship of Baalim. Her virgin girls and boys would sacrifice their virginity to the lustful worshipers of Baalim. Any babies born because of those orgies in so-called worship were used as sacred sacrifices to the idol. They were burned alive in the arms of the hollow statues. People of many nations were welcomed to have sexual pleasure in worship to those idols.

When Israel went to possess Canaan, she was told to destroy such and to cleanse the pollution from her land. However, Israel, little by little, began to take up the heathen sensuality and idolatry. Ezekiel 20 describes the lust of sensuality, which Israel brought from Egypt when she came out of that country from slavery. Verse 8 states that Israel did so. Verses 26-31 state that Israel offered her first-born children as sacrifices to be burned to idols in her high place of Bamah.

Ezekiel 23:19-20 states that Israel and Judah doted on her paramours in Egypt. (The prophet addressed a divided nation of Israel.) The definition of *paramours* is "male prostitutes." Ezekiel depicts Judah and Israel as lewd women, who had continuously practiced whoredoms since the founding of Israel as a nation. Israel had not cleansed herself of the practice of Nimrod's idolatry since having left Egyptian slavery long years before Ezekiel began to prophesy. Aaron contended with that at Sinai shortly after having left slavery. He made the worshipers of the Egyptian golden calf strip off their clothes to worship. Exodus 32:1-8, 21-25 recounts that Israel "played" naked around the calf. That form of so-called worship was very familiar to many in Israel who had been forced into degradation as slaves to Egyptian idolaters. All this gave rise to the need for the LORD to make such a demonstration in giving His commandments that He shook the mountain with fiery smoke, thunderous voice, and blasting of trumpets to convince Israel of His supremacy as Almighty God. However, the lust for sin calloused thousands of Israel at the base of the mountain that was quaking under the presence of God. Therefore, God's wrath fell upon Israel.

    God is never cruel or unjustified with harsh punishment. The misuse of the sacred privilege of pure worship to Almighty God and of the intimacy of marriage has always brought punishment upon those who desecrate and distort the right. Man is a living soul, and God does not tolerate His creation to go on forever desecrating worship or the God-given privilege of pleasure and procreation in marriage.

CHAPTER 2

EHUD, GOD'S SECOND NEVERTHELESS

It did not take long for Israel to forget history and her prior misery and servitude. Once again she yearned for the perverse worship to Baal, Ashtoreth, and the groves. Israel did evil in the sight of the LORD. The once beautiful vacation mecca of palm trees, the alluring city of pleasure, was attacked. The Amorites and Amalekites overwhelmed the city and killed everyone there. They moved in and set up housekeeping in the lap of luxury. That smarted Israel's ego. However, King Eglon of Moab was thought to be too powerful to be challenged. Once more Israel was forced into servitude for eighteen years because she had sinned against the LORD. In His great mercies, God sent another Nevertheless.

In the tribe of Benjamin lived a man named Gera, a grain farmer. Gera's son, Ehud, was noted for being left-handed. It seems the Scripture indicates there was more to the story of his being left-handed than merely that he predominantly used his left hand. Ehud had a handicap which forced him to become left-handed. The LORD raised Ehud up to deliver Israel. God used Ehud's handicap to Israel's advantage.

King Eglon of Moab had lived lavishly. He had

eaten from the bounty provided by Israel's servitude. He became a very obese man, used to daily naps in his sunbathed summer parlor under the palm trees. The royal summer palace was situated on the plains of Jordan River within the boundaries of the tribe of Benjamin. Ehud was quite familiar with the city of palm trees.

It was customary for Israelites to send presents to the ruling monarch. Eglon suspected nothing when Ehud arrived and announced that he had brought a gift for the king. "I've brought a present from your subjects to honor King Eglon," Ehud declared. Carrying the present conspicuously, Ehud was ushered into the presence of King Eglon. The representatives of Israel offered the presents with much pomp and flattery; then Ehud and his fellow ambassadors left. But courage stopped Ehud at the quarries of Gilgal. That landmark at Gilgal stirred the testimonial memory of how God had delivered Israel and had made a miraculous passage for Israel to cross Jordan.

Ehud returned to the palace and asked, "May I see the king? I have a message for him." The servants gave him passage into the summer parlor, where King Eglon was talking with some advisors. "I have a secret errand to report to you," Ehud whispered conspiratorially to the king. Eglon perked up, hoping to receive some juicy information of espionage. Ehud bowed respectfully.

"Keep silent!" Eglon commanded. He turned and spoke, "You men and servants are dismissed. This man and I have a private business matter." The advisors and the gaggle of servants bowed and melted into the corridors of the summer palace. "Please come to sit in the parlor, and close the door behind you," Eglon smiled at Ehud. "We will be alone." Ehud obeyed and faced King Eglon in the lavish summer parlor. A cool breeze wafted through the porch. Eglon had taken a seat on his cushioned tapestry lounge chair and relaxed. "Now, tell me what secret you have, Ehud." A smirk of superiority twitched his mouth into a condescending smile. A comical bulge of Eglon's fat eyes betrayed his impatience. Ehud took a seat and scooted to the edge of it. A slight bulge appeared in his cloak over his right thigh.

Before leaving home, Ehud had made himself a very sharp, double-edged dagger. He had it strapped and concealed on his right thigh under his cloak. He successfully smuggled it through security into the presence of the king. "I have a message from God unto you," Ehud said with no penchant for coddling. He stepped close as if to whisper the message. The handmade dagger was stealthily pulled from the sheath with Ehud's left hand, and with a powerful lunge Ehud plunged it into the king's fat belly. King Eglon had no time to cry out. Ehud tried to remove the dagger after stabbing the king, but the entire eighteen-inch blade and the handle were buried in layers of fat. Ehud left the dagger in the gushing stench of Eglon's severed bowel. Ehud quickly exited the door and locked it behind himself. He nonchalantly escaped by way of the porch and sprinted away with a dignified smile splitting his face.

King Eglon's attendants noted that Ehud was departing. "We'll check on our king to see if he needs anything before his afternoon nap." They tapped on the parlor door. No response came. They knocked a little louder and listened for a word. The silence raised no alarm or worry. "The door is locked. He must be asleep already. We'll return later when his nap is over. Leave him to his privacy." Much later the servants still could not rouse their master. They were ashamed that they had been absent in attending him for so long. "Get the key," one suggested. "There must be something wrong. The king will be terribly upset that we have not been here sooner." The parlor doors swung open, and the servants smelled the king before they saw him. Their eyes bulged in horror at the mound on the floor. They screamed and fled the room, calling for the royal guards. "King Eglon has fainted! He fell off his chair and is on the floor! We need help to lift him. Call the doctor."

    The guards and the doctor lifted the fat man's head. "He's dead," they affirmed. They lifted the body, and more dirt spilled on their shoes. "Must have ruptured his intestines from being too fat." After much heaving and strain, they got Eglon to his bed; then they discovered the dagger buried deeply in the fat king's abdomen. The inquiry began at once. "Who saw the king last?"

    "We did," the servants answered. "We ushered an Israelite messenger before King Eglon. The man had earlier brought a present and had left, but he returned with a secret message for our lord, King Eglon."

    "The king ordered us to leave them alone. We left as ordered and went about our work. Upon returning to the parlor, we found the door locked. We opened it and found this!"

Ehud, God's Second Nevertheless

"Who was that Israelite man?" the captain of the guards bellowed.

"He said his name was Ehud, from the tribe of Benjamin," one stammered.

"Pursue him!" the captain demanded. His orders were of none affect, for Ehud had already escaped to the Israelite city of Seirath.

Ehud quickly implemented a plan to attack Moab. He climbed the mountain in Ephraim and blew the trumpet to muster an army. The reverberating sound of the battle call echoed from the mountain. For miles around the Israelite men heard the urgent call. They left their families, their plows, their blacksmith forges, their fishing nets, and their harvest tools and strapped on their weapons. They assembled on the mountain. "King Eglon is dead!" Ehud declared. "I killed him! The Moabites are confused and unraveled. Let us strike them now before they recover. The LORD has given them into your hand." Ehud's wise faith declared that credit for victory belonged to the LORD and to the warriors. "Follow me," he said and led the army down the slopes to the fords of Jordan River. They waded in with a surprise attack and quickly overthrew the Moabite militia. Israel slew about ten thousand soldiers of Moab's elite military forces.

Judges 3:29-30 states that those Moabite soldiers were all lusty men of valor. None escaped. Moab was subdued, and Israel embarked on a period of eighty years of peace and rest.

According to I Chronicles 8:6-8, Ehud sent some tribal members to other cities of Benjamin and also to

Nevertheless, God

Moab to live. As was customary, a conquering ruler sent a number of his people to live in the conquered territory to govern it, to collect taxes, and to police the defeated people. The Israelites often raised their families in the adopted country and sometimes intermarried with the citizens of that country.

CHAPTER 3
SHAMGAR, THE PLOWMAN JUDGE

Along the Mediterranean Sea lay a vast strip of land that Israel had failed to conquer, known as Gaza, home to the Philistines. The Philistines were cruel and ruthless warriors. Some of them were descendants of giants. They were haters of Israel and never tried to make peace leagues with her. Open hostility and plunder by those Philistines always vexed Israel. When Israel forsook the LORD, the Philistines took back much of the hard-won territory in the southwest part of Israel. Israel's national security was precarious. Threats of the fierce warriors spread across the land.

Word reached Shamgar, the son of Anath. His was a farming family. They plowed their fields with oxen. Shamgar's righteous anger boiled at the news of Philistine threats. He had no weapons of war with which to fight. Shamgar was no skilled swordsman. He had no bow and arrows or spears and shields, but he had the LORD God of Israel and knew how to use the long, sharp stick he had so often used to prod his oxen to pull the plow across the family's farmland. The goad stick was used to poke the hindquarters of stubborn or slothful animals. The goad controlled the oxen and taught them to obey the driver's commands. The goad was also used as a weapon of defense against wild animals, which

Nevertheless, God

sometimes attacked and killed or maimed farm animals. It took skill, strength, and patience to master the use of a goad.

Shamgar was qualified in every respect in the use of an ox goad. When the Philistine warriors marched forces onto his farm, Shamgar fiercely defended his freedom and his home. Alone he attacked the six hundred Philistines who intruded daringly on his land. Slicing the air with the stout pole, Shamgar began to knock off man after man until all six hundred warriors lay dead around him. Again Israel was delivered from oppression.

Chapter 4
Deborah: a Mother, a Judge

Deborah was a prophetess, married to Lapidoth. They lived in a very rural area between Ramah and Bethel. A palm tree planted in Deborah's name stood at her home. That tree was a landmark to identify her house. The meaning of the name, Deborah, denotes that she kept bees. A bee farmer would of necessity live in the country away from crowds and among vineyards, fruit trees, and vegetable farms. Deborah was also a mother in Israel. The people of Israel went to her house to be judged. Judges, chapters 4 and 5 tell her story.

It would seem that once or twice repeating a lesson would have made the learning permanent in practice, but Israel's memory and lust for sin made her a poor student. History repeated itself again when Israel did evil in the sight of the LORD. After the eighty years of rest by the deliverance brought by Ehud and Shamgar, Israel caused God to sell her into bondage.

God sold her to Jabin, a Canaanite king. Jabin had conquered Israel with an iron force. He mightily oppressed Israel. His war machines were chariots of iron. Those extraordinary machines of mutilation and horror had sharp knives welded on the spokes of the wheels. Those sliced and maimed the legs of horses and men as the chariots plowed among Israel's forces. The chariots

Nevertheless, God

were pulled by fast steeds lusting for the battle. Not only were the chariots weapons themselves, but they were also excellent shields for archers and spearmen. Israel was terrified, frozen in fear. Israel in weakness submitted to Jabin and his mighty military captain, Sisera, who encamped in Harosheth. For twenty years Israel suffered the shame and humiliation of Jabin's mastery.

    Deborah described the situation in which her people existed. Judges 5 states that Israel had deserted the highways and had to walk the back trails and byways to avoid Sisera's chariots patrolling the highways. Evidently Israel either had no horses to ride or could not risk riding horses because they had to walk on hidden trails and footpaths for safety. The villagers had fled to walled cities to escape the plundering villains. Israel had chosen new gods and constantly did battle in her city gates. All shields and spears had been confiscated. Israel had manpower but possessed no weapons for warfare. She mustered forty thousand soldiers but had nothing to equip them for battle. When the people went to draw water from their community wells, the enemy archers shot at them. Water became an expensive, rationed, and stolen commodity. However, at those water wells and springs, Israel began to talk about the righteous acts of the LORD toward the villagers in Israel. Rumblings of revival and repentance swept across enemy lines and penetrated the armored, patrolled borders of enemy territory to reach thousands of Israel with the message of hope.

    Such was the terrible state of Israel. Deborah said the corruption existed until "I arose a mother in Israel."

Deborah: a Mother, a Judge

Deborah could not ignore the right for her children's freedom. She knew that deliverance could and would come if Israel returned to repentance toward God and obeyed His Word. She lived in the rural area of Israel and understood the harassment and danger the villagers had suffered, but she refused to be driven into a walled city, where she could not take care of her family business of bee farming. Somehow she communicated her zeal and faith to the governors of Israel. They caught the faith and believed her message. The town of Machir on the east side of Jordan in the tribe of Manasseh had sent governors to the meetings. The tribe of Zebulun had sent scribes to write the minutes and to report and publish the decisions. Those leaders left Deborah's home with a zeal to do something for their God and their people. The princes of Issachar remained with Deborah to assist in organizing the rebellion against Jabin. The other tribes went about their business as if deliverance meant nothing to them. They had sent no ambassadors, nor did they give any assistance to promote the insurrection.

The governors of the federated tribes of Israel rode on white mules, the status of authority, but they had to ride secretively. Word spread that the governors were holding town meetings in the city gates. The cities always held court and large public gatherings inside their main gates. That was like a city hall and municipal building for all legal and public matters. Those governors began to preach faith in the LORD God of Israel from city to city. The tribe of Ephraim had a small but strong group of men who were willing to oppose King Jabin,

Nevertheless, God

the Amalekite monarch. The men of Benjamin joined the mustering troops. Plans were made for the marshaling of Israelite men to launch an offense against Jabin.

God told Deborah that Barak of the city of Kedesh in Naphtali was to lead Israel's army. Barak was at home talking to God about the plight of Israel. However, he was reluctant to declare his burden and call. When the message from Deborah arrived at his door, Barak received confirmation that God had indeed chosen him. Reluctance still niggled at his conscious fears. Deborah's orders were: "Go toward Mount Tabor with ten thousand men from the tribes of Naphtali and Zebulun. God said, 'I will draw Sisera to the Kishon River. Captain Sisera of King Jabin's army with his chariots of iron will be delivered into your hand.'"

Barak replied, "If you will go with me, Deborah, I will go. If you will not go with me, I refuse to go."

Deborah pledged her support and presence but gave the prophecy: "Barak, this journey will not be for your honor. Because of your reluctance, God will deliver Sisera into the hand of a woman." Deborah packed her gear and went to Kedesh. She marched with Barak up Mount Tabor, but Barak had to take charge of the mustering of troops. Mount Tabor was the ideal location for gathering Israel's warriors. The mountain was a predominant peak in the tribe of Naphtali on the converging borders of three tribes—Issachar, Naphtali, and Zebulun. From the peaks of Mount Tabor, Barak blew the call. Amazingly, the men came. Ten thousand men gathered around Barak and Deborah. They received instructions

Deborah: a Mother, a Judge

and the Word of God to assure them of victory against Jabin's strong, superior army.

In the plains of Zaanaim near Kedesh, a small group of Bedouins made camp. Those were Kenites of the descendants of Moses' father-in-law, Jethro. Heber had split with the Kenites, who were of the children of Hobab, Moses' brother-in-law. Hobab had joined the ranks of Israel and had provided them valuable information about the land in the wilderness east of Jordan River. He took his family across the river with Israel and enjoyed the safety and protection under Israel's banner.

One of the Kenites became disgruntled with his relatives and separated from the clan. He moved his tent to the plains of Zaanaim near Kedesh, the home of Barak. However, when Israel fell to Jabin's forces, Heber turned traitor to Israel. He had been a part of the Kenites and had joined ranks with Israel but had never been converted to becoming indivisible with her. He remained a nomad, moving his herd of cattle at will, independent of his relatives and everyone else. Heber sought advantage with Sisera because Heber had a peace agreement with Jabin, the king. Heber observed the movement of men on foot headed to Mount Tabor. He had heard the bugle call to muster and reported to Sisera, "Barak has gone to Mount Tabor with ten thousand Israelites to launch an attack against Jabin."

"Thank you, Heber." Sisera flashed a warm smile. "I assure you full protection and liberty in exchange for this information." Sisera's chariot rolled down the road beside Heber's camp. He chuckled as he briskly urged his steed forward to the military compound at Harosheth. His nine hundred chariots of iron and the fierce steeds and warriors were well prepared to crush a rebellion. The gates of the fortress swung open, and the mighty Sisera drove through in a rush to muster his own forces. "The Israelites have mustered an army for an attack. Make ready your weapons. Harness the horses. Make ready the chariots for battle!" The clanging of metal and neighing horses made music for Jabin's ears. The war whoops of Sisera's capable warriors sent thrilling shivers of pride down his back. Jabin had complete confidence in Sisera's military superiority and strategies for victory in any battle. He relaxed and smiled.

Sisera kissed his mother and promised to return with beautiful treasures for her. "I'll crush those Israelites like swatting flies," he boasted. "Israel has no weapons and certainly none that can stop my chariots of iron. We'll easily take everything Israel has for a spoil and make them our slaves. I intend to catch me a few pretty girls for my own pleasure as well," Sisera bragged as he again kissed his mother good-bye.

Barak led his foot soldiers down the slopes of Tabor. In the Kishon Valley below the mountain, Sisera had his forces entrenched, waiting for Israel's bedraggled army to walk into the snare. In amazement they saw the forces of nature gathering a torrential storm, which without warning burst upon the whole Kishon Valley. The river instantly became a raging, writhing beast of destruction crashing down from the mountain heights and devastating everything in its path. Iron chariots cannot float. Neither can horses that are harnessed to iron chariots swim. Sisera's soldiers were forced to abandon their comfortable seats and weapons to flee for their lives. The forces of battle were equalized. Both armies were on foot. Both had few if any weapons with which to fight. The wall of water chased the enemy and swallowed many of them. By the time Israel reached the staging ground for battle, the Kishon River had become a beast. Israel pursued the enemy that had escaped, and the slaughter began. The LORD God of Israel fought with weapons beyond human control.

The earth trembled in that clash of nature. Sisera saw the plight of his army. His own chariot was useless. He abandoned his troops and fled on foot into the plains away from the river. He kept running at top pace for Heber's tent. *I'll find safety there,* he thought. Then he heard the sound of running behind him. Glancing over his shoulder, he recognized the runner to be an Israelite soldier. Adrenalin pumped a burst of speed. He did not slow his gallop until he burst into the well-defined yard around Heber's tent.

Heber was not at home. His wife, Jael, had milked the cows and had poured the milk into bottles to cool in the breeze in the shade. The cream had been separated and churned into butter. She had sculptured it into a beautiful form and had put it in her most elegant dish. With her morning chores done, she waited for her husband to arrive for lunch. Jael heard the sound of running. She stepped from her tent to see who was so urgently approaching. It was not Heber she saw. She recognized the

Nevertheless, God

garments of Captain Sisera. The man jumped the hedgerow surrounding the small meadow where the milk cows were grazing. He gasped for breath and stopped in front of Jael's door.

"Captain Sisera!" Jael greeted. "Come inside, and refresh yourself. You look as if you've run from the devil. You have no need to fear in this home."

Still panting from the hard run, Sisera stepped inside the shade of the tent and nodded with a smile. "Thanks," he managed to say.

Jael cautiously looked around to see if anyone else may have seen her unorthodox invitation. No one lurked within sight. Jael entered the tent behind her guest and gushed in a most beguiling tone, "Sit and relax. Rest for a while. Heber will be home very soon." Then she smiled hospitably and asked, "May I prepare you a drink?"

"Of course. I knew I could count on Heber to help me," Sisera responded. "May I have a drink of water?"

"Yes, but I can get you something more nourishing than water. There is fresh buttermilk or sweet milk already cooled. Also, I'll bring you some freshly churned butter and some fresh bread."

"I promise that you will be greatly rewarded for your service to King Jabin's cause," Sisera offered. Jael served the food in her best china. Sisera ate the bread and butter and gulped the milk. He immediately began to feel the muscles relax, and he nodded.

"You must be very tired, Captain," Jael said.

Sisera jerked his head in a snort and blushed. "Jael, please stand guard in the tent door. If anybody

Deborah: a Mother, a Judge

comes to ask if some man is here, tell him, 'No.' I do embarrassingly admit that I am very tired."

"Relax. I'll cover you with this blanket. No one will know that you are sleeping here."

Sisera grinned a tired, lopsided grin. "I will report your kindness to King Jabin," he said with a yawn. "If I do fall asleep, I hope I do not disturb the peace with my snoring."

"There will be enough noise around here to disguise any snores," Jael assured. "I usually make lots of noise stretching tent ropes and staking them to the ground. In fact, I need to get that job done before Heber gets home. I'll leave you to your nap." The woman threw the blanket over the prone figure of Sisera, the mighty captain. He already was in a deep sleep. Jael smiled and left the tent. She listened to the soft purring of the man sprawled on the floor of her home. She felt apprehensive about the situation, yet an unexplainable daring directed her to do something. Quietly she took a tent stake and a sledgehammer and crept into her tent. She positioned the stake over Sisera's temple, and with one powerful blow of the hammer, she drove that stake through the skull and pinned Sisera to the ground. The mighty captain never knew what had hit him.

The sound of another runner alerted Jael. Thinking it might be her husband, she rushed out the tent door to meet the person. As before, she did not see Heber but this time recognized an Israelite warrior. "Barak! You are surely pursuing Sisera. My husband, Heber, was the informant for Sisera about your army and where he

Nevertheless, God

would find you. He also advised that the battle should be staged by the Kishon River. And now you must come to see the man for whom you are looking." Jael led the way through the tent door and beckoned Barak inside. "There," she said as she removed the blanket from the pinioned body. "Sisera came into my home asking for a drink of water and that he might rest. He fell asleep after eating a snack and drinking warm milk. So I nailed him." Jael clutched her robe and trembled. "I could not have anyone charge me with being unfaithful to my husband. Heber is gone, and I was home alone. Sisera, the mighty captain, could have easily taken advantage of my situation. He is known for his disrespect for women. As you see, God spared me shame and helped me to kill him."

"You had every right to defend yourself, Jael," Barak answered. "You did the right thing. All of Israel shall sing of your feat. Today, Israel has been liberated from the oppression of King Jabin and his mighty army. This day the warriors of Israel have received help from the LORD to destroy Jabin's army completely."

Meanwhile, Sisera's proud mother lolled about her lavish apartment, boasting of her son's victory. Every now and again she arose to peer through the lattice screening her window. The day wore thin, and she grew worried. "Why is Sisera's chariot so long in returning?" she cried. "Why has there been no message from the battle?"

"Your ladyship, quit worrying," her wise ladies answered. "Sisera's army has easily won the victory. As we speak, they are dividing the spoil and the captives."

Deborah: a Mother, a Judge

The haughty mother talked to herself to reinforce her assumptions. "Of course. I can almost see the gorgeous raiments embroidered with the finest needlework that Sisera will bring home. You know, the Israelites can produce the most beautiful embroidery. It is so exquisite that both sides of the material appear the same!"

"Certainly, your ladyship!" the attendants soothed.

"I am sure Sisera has captured enough pretty girls to give each of his men a couple for his pleasure. Those girls can produce royal robes for all Sisera's warriors," she exuded. She and her ladies waited through that day and night before word reached her.

Sisera's mother was excited to answer the knock on her door. "Oh, this must be the news I have been expecting!" She stared into the eyes of a scared, weary man, whose face portrayed the story.

"Sisera is dead! So is our entire army! We've lost everything in a flash flood of the Kishon River and by the sword of the Israelite army." The messenger left the woman to her tears and humiliation.

While the Canaanites lamented their defeat, Deborah and Barak joined all of Israel in a victory song and worshiped the LORD. Revival swept across the land. For forty years Israel remained faithful to the LORD. Deborah had proclaimed, "I, a mother in Israel, arose when I saw our highways deserted and travelers walking through byways. I remembered the God of Sinai. Our LORD God of Israel is a man of war!"

CHAPTER 5

GIDEON, ISRAEL'S MAN OF VALOR

When Jabin, Sisera, Deborah, and Barak became lost in the annals of Israel's history, her people fell into the old lust for sin, and God delivered Israel into the hand of Midian. Midian was the son of Abraham by his second wife, Keturah. Abraham had married Keturah several years after his first wife, Sarah, had died and Isaac, their son, had been married and received his inheritance as Abraham's acknowledged heir. Keturah's boys had been given lavish gifts and sent away from Abraham and Isaac before Abraham died. That act fostered much resentment and hatred toward Isaac and his family (Genesis 25:1-6).

Hundreds of years had passed, and both Midian and Isaac had produced many descendants. Midian had become an established nation. Israel also became an established nation in the very territory in which Abraham had lived. Midian's age-old resentment and hatred simmered as he never desired reconciliation with his brother's descendants. When Israel turned her back on God, the LORD allowed the festering grudge which Midian harbored to rupture into retribution. The Midianites swamped Israel with plundering bands of warriors. They made life unbearable for Israel. Many Israelites fled into the mountains, where they lived in caves or dens and fortified strongholds. They came out at night to gather food and to work their fields (Judges 6:1-6).

When the spring crops were ready for harvest, Midian allied with Amalek and others of the east to raid and to plunder the fields of Israel. Israel's food supply was confiscated by her enemies. Across the countryside, Israel suffered deprivation. Her fields were robbed all the way to Gaza, where the Philistines lived. The Midianites raided the barns, the pastures, and the folds, stealing the sheep, oxen, donkeys, and herds of cattle. The hordes of enemy raiders drove Israel's flocks before them as they advanced like an army of grasshoppers devouring everything in its path. In the wake, Israel was left impoverished and literally starving. The numberless army of the plundering enemy and their camels of war covered the land with their tents and the horror and terror of life.

The plight Israel suffered awakened her to repentance. Her people began to cry for God to deliver them from their tormentors. The LORD sent a prophet, who preached a sermon from Israel's history (Judges 6:8-10): "Thus saith the LORD God of Israel, I brought you up from Egypt, and brought you forth out of the house of bondage; and I delivered you out of the hand of the Egyptians, and out of the hand of all that oppressed you. I drove them out from before you. I gave you their land. I said to you, I am the LORD your God. Fear not the gods of the Amorites, in whose land you dwell. But you have not obeyed my voice." The challenge of that unnamed

Gideon, Israel's Man of Valor

prophet roused Israel to repent even more. They revived the stories of God's miracles performed in the past.

In the tribe of Manasseh, among the oak trees of Ophrah, a farmer named Joash had a small, secluded wheat field from which his youngest son, Gideon, had secreted the harvest. Gideon had hidden the grain by the winepress. God sent an angel to that farm. He sat under an oak and watched Gideon hiding by the winepress and threshing wheat. Gideon kept a cautious watch for the Midianites as he beat the precious grain from the stalks and husk. Gideon had heard the prophet's message and was pondering his words. He questioned why Israel had forsaken God. He wondered why God had allowed horrendous atrocities to happen to His people. As he meditated, he beat the grain, hoping to get enough to feed his family for the day. The angel observed for some time before he appeared to Gideon. The angel suddenly became visible, startling Gideon. "The LORD is with you, you mighty man of valor!" the angel spoke.

Gideon stuttered in astonishment, "Oh my Lord, if the LORD is with us, why has all this impoverishment and oppression happened to us? Where are all God's miracles of which our fathers told us? They say the LORD brought us up from Egypt, but now He has forsaken us. He has delivered us into the hands of the Midianites."

With a knowing, kind look, the LORD spoke to Gideon, "Go in this your might. You shall save Israel from the hands of Midian. I have sent you."

In shock and confusion, Gideon replied, "With what shall I save Israel? My family is poor, and I am the

Nevertheless, God

least in my father's house. I have no qualifications to lead Israel."

The LORD spoke again, "Surely I will be with you. You shall smite the Midianites as one man."

Reality began to dawn upon Gideon that the man before him was not an ordinary human. He suspected that the man was of supernatural origin and addressed him as such, "If I have found grace and favor in your eyes, show me a sign that You are talking to me. Are You a mirage? Are You a dream of my wishful imagination? If You are truly real, don't go away. I'll be back with a present for You." Gideon waited for an answer.

"I will wait as you have asked," the LORD replied.

Gideon bolted from the spot. He ran to kill one of the baby goats he had hidden from the marauders. As the meat boiled, he had unleavened cakes made from the measure of flour he had ground. This was to have been food for his family, but Gideon was emboldened to believe that if the LORD had really appeared to him, the LORD would also feed his family. When the food was cooked, Gideon lifted the meat from the pot into a basket. He poured the broth into a nice pan and gathered the bread. He returned to the winepress. He thought, *If that man is really from God, I have nothing to lose even if he eats it all. If he is not of God, dinner is already prepared for my family, and I merely have had an hallucination.* The visitor waited by the oak tree by the winepress as Gideon presented the food with a sigh of relief.

The angel of the LORD said, "Put the meat and bread on this rock. Pour out the broth." Gideon obeyed.

Then the angel extended his staff so the end of it touched the meat and bread. The rock burst into a consuming flame. Gideon jumped back in awe. As he watched, the angel disappeared as vapor in the wind.

Gideon trembled in amazement, anguish, and fear. "What sorrow, O Lord GOD, for I have seen an angel of the LORD face to face!" he stammered.

The voice of the LORD spoke again to Gideon, "Peace be to you. Don't be afraid; you won't die." This quieted Gideon's nerves. His thundering heart settled into a steady thumping. He contemplated what he should do next. He gathered natural stones around the rock upon which fire had consumed the food. There he made an altar unto the LORD.

"This altar shall be called JEHOVAH-SHALOM, for God has given peace," Gideon declared. Gideon's altar remained a monument dedicated to God for years.

After dark, Gideon ruminated over his encounter, and the LORD spoke to him again, "Take your father's young bullock and the seven-year-old bullock, and tear down the altar of Baal that your father has built. Cut down the grove he planted and dedicated to Baal. Build an altar unto the LORD thy God upon the top of the rock in the prepared place. Kill the second bullock, and burn it as a sacrifice upon the altar. Use the wood of the grove to burn it."

Gideon took ten of his menservants to help him. Under cover of darkness, they harnessed the oxen to pull down Baal's altar and to snake out the logs to be cut.

The men chopped the trees and killed the bullock.

Nevertheless, God

When it was placed upon the massive rock, they piled the hewn trees around the rock and atop the bullock. By dawn, the task was done, and nothing remained of the sacred place to Baal. The aroma of roasting meat filled the air. The smoke and smell wafted over the tree stumps and into the awareness of the growling stomachs of the villagers. Gideon and his men beat the sun's announcement of day and had stolen back home. Gideon avoided his father and his household. "We must not let my father catch us," he told his servants. The tired but exhilarated men crept to their beds about the time the villagers began to stir. The smoke and smell of roasting meat drew the folk to Joash's worship center.

An angry, disdainful cry reverberated from the hill of blazing coals around the rock altar. The villagers had assembled, thinking to have morning prayers to Baal and to eat flesh from his altar. "Who has done such horrible, shameful things to our sanctuary?" they squawked. They shouted, "O Baal, we have come to worship you." In astonishment they vowed, "Someone has desecrated your sacred place, and we shall find and execute whoever did this!" They began to inquire first at Joash's house. They banged furiously on the door. An extensive investigation revealed that Gideon was the culprit. "Bring out your son Gideon. We will kill him for throwing down the altar to Baal and for cutting down his grove," they demanded, raising their fists in defiance.

Surprisingly, Joash did not recoil before the men. Instead he yelled, "All of you listen and listen well. Why are you pleading for Baal? Will you save him? Those

Gideon, Israel's Man of Valor

who plead for Baal, let them be put to death this morning. If Baal is god, let him speak for himself. He should plead for himself because someone tore down his altar, Jerubbaal!" Joash slammed the door with that threat. He posted armed servants at each door and window.

The mob grumbled but began to disperse. "We shall report this to the Midianites. You'll pay. Wait and see," they guffawed. The sound of galloping hooves clattered on the road to the Midianite post. "Jerubbaal!" they bellowed. "We have a contender with Baal!"

The ire of wrath boiled quickly. Both Midian and Amalek had always enjoyed a good boxing match with the wimps of Israel. "But with some idiot desecrating our god, we'll do more than ruffle a few feathers. We'll wipe out the whole henhouse and all the chickens in it!" they mocked. The military swarmed to the chosen battlefield. The mass of horses, camels, cattle, and food wagons ushered the armies to the valley of Jezreel, the long, wide plain that by nature beckoned armies to stage battle.

Gideon heard the angry threats of the idolaters. He prayed to the LORD while the smoldering ruins of Baal's sanctuary polluted the air around his home. The Spirit of the LORD came upon him, and he blew a trumpet to muster his kinfolk to fan through Israel with word to arm themselves for an attack. He dispatched messengers to the tribes of Manasseh, Asher, Zebulun, and Naphtali. Thirty-two thousand men gathered to meet Jerubbaal, the brave one who dared to defy Baal and brought threats of the wrath of Midian.

Gideon watched the Israelites stealthily gathering.

Nevertheless, God

His heart trembled at their sheepish fear. He began questioning his own decision. He prayed again, "God, if You will save Israel by my hand like You said, confirm it to me by this sign: I'll put a fleece of wool in the floor. If You really will use me, let the fleece be wet with dew but all the ground around it be dry in the morning." Gideon spread the fleece and went to bed. He slept fitfully. At dawn he checked the fleece. He picked up the soaked fleece and wrung out a bowl of dew distilled only on the fleece. He kicked up dust from the ground around it. He refreshed himself with the water. But that was not the conclusive sign for Gideon. In his evening prayer he asked God, "Don't be hot in anger with me, but I must do one more test. If You really will deliver Israel by my hand, prove it by letting the fleece be dry overnight and let the ground around it be wet with dew."

Gideon was not unknowledgeable of fleeces. A wet fleece does not dry very quickly. In fact, his fleece probably was still damp from the previous night. Therefore it was no simple matter that he asked of God. The night passed, and Gideon woke to check the fleece. It was bone dry! He sloughed in mud all around it. His faith thermometer rose to the highest level. "I believe God!" he yelled. "The LORD God will deliver Israel from Midian!" Reveille called the men to assemble for orders.

Before the day ended, Israel's men had made camp at the well of Harod. The fountain was just south of the Midianite camp by the hill of Moreh in the valley of Jezreel (Judges 7:1). There at the fountain, God spoke to Gideon. God perceived the nervous fear that gripped many of the men who followed Gideon. "Gideon, there are too many men with you. I will not give the Midianites into your hand with so many men. Israel would vaunt herself against Me saying, 'My own hand saved me.' Send those who are fearful home. I cannot use men who are full of fear to deliver Israel."

Gideon made the proclamation, and, amazingly, twenty-two thousand men packed their gear and left the camp. Gideon shook his head. "Only ten thousand remain, LORD!"

"Yes, I know, Gideon. But you still have too many men. Bring them to the water. I will try them there for you. I shall tell you the ones I choose to go with you and who will not."

Gideon called the men to the large fountain of springing water. Evidently, that was an artesian fountain, which formed the headwaters for a stream coming from the mountain south of the Jezreel Valley. The men were tired and thirsty after having trooped down Mount Tabor and into the valley. They fell on their bellies and gulped water like animals.

However, a few did not fall to the ground but rather scooped up water with their hands and drank. Those men watched for the enemy as they quenched their thirst. The LORD spoke, "The men who scooped water with their hands to drink are to be separated from the others." The men formed two groups. Nine thousand and seven hundred acknowledged that they had drunk water on their bellies. Three hundred huddled in the other group. God spoke, "The nine thousand seven hundred

Nevertheless, God

men are to go home. The three hundred are to stay with Gideon." Gideon watched his army march into the distance on the road to their homes.

Gideon turned to the small band of men and said, "Pack your food and a trumpet for each of you. Prepare to march at a moment's notice. When God speaks, we must obey instantly." The three hundred men eagerly followed orders and waited with Gideon until evening prayers. Under the blackness of night, prayer was made, interceding for direction for battle. "We've done all You have said, God. We are so few in number that I'm skeptical. How on earth am I to attack Midian's vast army and expect to win?"

God responded, "Gideon, get up, and go down to the Midianite host; for I have delivered it into your hand. But if you are afraid to go down, take your servant, Phurah, and you two go alone. You shall hear what the enemy says. Afterward, your hands will be strengthened to go with your army to the host."

Unceremoniously, Gideon left his three hundred men in camp. He and Phurah slipped into the darkness. They cautiously surveyed the enemy from the height above the tents of the Midianite camp. "Look, Phurah; as far as you can see along the valley there is an innumerable multitude of them!" Gideon pointed to the moon-splashed Jezreel Valley.

"Looks like a swarm of grasshoppers dropped into the valley," Phurah whispered. "Look at their camels! They have as many camels as soldiers."

"Let's slip down to their outer ranks and listen.

Those camped on the outer ring of the camp are the first responders in battle. They will know the battle plans for attack. We shall listen to their discussion." Gideon motioned for Phurah to follow him.

Crouching, the two men crept near the first pair of sentinels. Hiding in the shadows, they paused at the sound of conversation. "I had a dream," one voice said.

"What was it?" another asked. "You have to tell it to keep me awake."

"I dreamed that a cake of barley bread tumbled into the host of Midian and came unto a tent. It smote the tent, knocking it down. It overturned the tent and strewed it along the ground," the dreamer said. "What do you think it means?"

The tent mate responded with the interpretation: "This barley cake is surely nothing else but the sword of Gideon, the son of Joash, a man of Israel. Into his hand has God delivered Midian and all this host."

The dreamer replied, "Gideon was who tore down the image of Baal and destroyed his sanctuary! We are in trouble!" The man panicked.

Gideon and Phurah heard that conversation very clearly. Gideon worshiped the LORD there in the shadow of death. Silently and sincerely he worshiped. With elation of spirit and belief in God, the two men dodged sleeping camels and slipped from the Midianite camp. They returned to their own men before midnight. By the light of the moon, Gideon gave instructions to his band of soldiers, "Watch me. Whatever I do, you do the same. When I blow the trumpet, all that are with me and you others blow your trumpets; then yell, 'The sword of the LORD and of Gideon!' Each of you carry a water pitcher and a burning torch. Cover the torch with your pitcher, and divide yourselves into three equal groups. Position yourselves as a group on a different peak around this valley. When we are in position, I will give the signal. In unison break your pitchers, blow the trumpets, and shout, for the LORD has given us victory!"

In the valley of Jezreel, the Midianite guards had just changed watch. The fresh sentinels, not anticipating any threat to their mighty forces, slouched carelessly into position. They played carefree games, drank, and told jokes as men of leisure do. They did not suspect that their enemy was positioning itself for a surprise attack.

Gideon took a hundred of his men with him, down the mountain slope, and stole into the perimeters of the Midianite camp. He waited until the others had positioned themselves on the surrounding hilltops. He lifted his trumpet in his right hand and broke the pitcher covering the torch in his left hand. He blew the call for the battle charge. The other men stationed on the surrounding peaks did the same as Gideon and those with him. In unison they cried, "The sword of the LORD and of Gideon!"

The shattering sound of three hundred breaking pitchers magnified by echoes from the mountains around the valley mingled with the sound of a charging army. Startled, the Midianite army leaped from their beds and grabbed their weapons. They saw their camp surrounded with fiery torches, many of which were just outside the camp. Tents were torched, and pandemonium ensued. The continual trumpet sound to charge echoed from the mountains, amplifying the sound. The Midianites spilled from their tents and began to slice their swords at the perceived invaders. They did not realize in the darkness that they were slaughtering their own troops still dressed in their pajamas. As the continuing declaration bounced from the mountain peaks and from Gideon's men on the edge of the camp, the fear of the sword of the LORD and of Gideon fell like swift destruction upon Israel's enemy. The Israelites watched transfixed as their enemy slaughtered each other. A few of the enemy escaped to Beth-shittah in Zererath. Some fled to the border of Abel-meholah and unto Tabbath. Word spread to the Israelite tribes that the host of Midian was in battle among themselves and that some were scattered in flight. Men from the tribes of Naphtali, Asher, and Manasseh took arms and pursued the enemy.

Gideon sent a post to Mount Ephraim: "Come down against the Midianites and take the waters of Beth-barah and Jordan before the enemy arrives." The men of Ephraim quickly obeyed. They stopped the fleeing Midianite officers. Prince Oreb and Prince Zeeb hastened to escape across Jordan River. The Ephraimites killed both princes. Their royal heads were ferried across the river and taken to Gideon.

After the dust of battle had settled and swords were returned to their scabbards, the Ephraimites filed charges against Gideon. "You are prejudiced against our tribe. Why have you served us such notice merely to

Nevertheless, God

patrol the waters of Beth–barah and Jordan? Why did you not call us to help in the fight against Midian?"

To the sharp chiding, Gideon answered, "What have I done in comparison to you? You've killed Oreb and Zeeb. God delivered them into your hands. What have I done to compare?" His wise answer defused the hot temper and cooled the wrath.

Gideon then passed over Jordan River in his pursuit of the fleeing Midianites. He and his three hundred men had been chasing their enemy all night. They had not eaten or rested in their determination to catch the Midianites. The angry dispute with Ephraim delayed the progress but did not stop them. They arrived in Succoth, an ancient camp east of Jordan where Jacob had made booths for his flocks and had built himself a home many years before. Gideon expected kind hospitality from the people of Succoth. "Please give my men some loaves of bread. They are faint and weary, for we have been pursuing Zebah and Zalmunna, the kings of Midian." He was shocked at their indignant response.

The men of Succoth sneered, "Are Zebah and Zalmunna already in your captivity that we should give you bread? We are not risking our necks by offending the Midianites. You know they have rule over us and can make life very miserable for offenders." The ignorance of Gideon's call, of his anointing, and of God's promise for deliverance did not excuse those men. They had the historical record of divine intervention for Israel, but they refused to believe victory was imminent for Gideon.

The mere fact that Gideon was chasing those

kings should have made the Israelites of Succoth rejoice. Succoth should have joined the effort but rather chose to remain passive, indifferent, and comfortable in their slave mentality. Gideon spat out his disgust through his teeth, "When the LORD has delivered those kings into my hand, I will return here. I will tear your flesh with the thorns of the wilderness and with briers."

He stormed away and went to Penuel, where he again asked for food. The evil men of Penuel rebuffed Gideon and his men as had those of Succoth. Penuel was the historical site where Jacob wrestled with an angel of God all night and had been given the name Israel. That experience had altered the course of history for Jacob's descendants. However, Penuel had sunk to such a level of unbelief that history and hundreds-of-years-old tradition meant nothing to them. The small army of Israelites were extremely hungry and bone weary but refused to be deterred from their pursuit. Gideon spat out a warning as his men left the city, "When I return, I will break down your tower."

It had been a thirty-mile chase without food or rest, but Gideon pressed on.

The Midianites had retreated to Karkor. Karkor was a secure fortress. The Midianites felt smug and secure within the protective walls and bulwarks of Karkor. Their fifteen thousand surviving troops had camped in Jezreel Valley among an innumerable host, but the regrouping and assessment of casualties revealed their loss to be one hundred and twenty thousand swordsmen who had killed each other in Gideon's phantom attack.

Nevertheless, God

The little band of persistent Israelite soldiers persevered, determined to catch and to defeat their foes. Gideon and his men went to Karkor by way of two small hamlets of tent dwellers in the tribe of Gad. From that vantage point east of Nobah and Jogbehah, Gideon advanced his attack on Midian. They killed most of the enemy forces, but the kings, Zebah and Zalmunna, fled again. Gideon was off on another tedious pursuit. Shortly afterward, the kings were captured. Before the sun rose, Gideon and his small army had discomfited the whole host of Midian.

With the two Midianite kings in tow astride their camels, Gideon and his men returned to Succoth. They caught a young man of Succoth and interrogated him. Their captive squealed under the pressure. He described the princes and elders of Succoth, all sixty-seven of them. Gideon bravely entered the city and rounded up those mockers. "Look. Here are the kings of Midian, Zebah and Zalmunna. These are the kings with which you reproached me, refusing to give bread to my men. I'm back as I promised to teach you a lesson." Gideon's soldiers herded those sixty-seven leaders of Succoth to the wilderness to teach them the lesson no one would forget. In the wilderness grew thorn bushes, which had very long, hard thorns, usually used for fencing cattle or sheep. Thick briers also grew in the wilderness. Gideon, as a farmer, was very familiar with those thorns and briers. He no doubt had used such for fencing the animals on the family farm. Such fences were the forerunner of barbed wire. Gideon braided thorns in with the long vines of briers. Those men were stripped naked and were forced to run through the gauntlet of soldiers, who used those whips of vines laced with hard, spike-like thorns to beat those sixty-seven men.

From Succoth, Gideon made his return trip to Penuel. The tower there was beaten down and the men of the city were killed, as Gideon had promised a few days before. With those two promises to Succoth and Penuel taken care of, Gideon turned his attention to his captives, whom he had kept alive as proof of his accomplishment in delivering Israel from Midian's oppression. A thorough inquisition of the two kings brought a startling confession, "We attacked Tabor after we learned that Baal's sanctuary had been destroyed and the groves had been burned. We killed the men there."

"Describe the men you killed," Gideon demanded.

"They looked like you, children of a king," the two indignant kings replied.

Gideon's anger boiled. "They were my brothers! If you had not killed them, I would have let you live. But since you murdered my mother's children, I will kill you!" Among Gideon's few warriors was his oldest son, Jether. Gideon knew the custom of honoring a worthy warrior with the right to kill the ruler of the conquered foe. That was like upgrading that warrior's rank. "Jether, get up and slay them," Gideon ordered.

Jether knew the implications of accepting the challenge and also the responsibilities which would fall upon him if he obeyed. "I'm too young. I'm afraid to accept that, Father," he stammered. He would not draw his sword as an indication of consideration.

Zebah and Zalmunna, the Midianite kings, relished the timidity of Gideon's son. They taunted Gideon with the idea that his family was not as fierce and brave as he had thought. "Get up and kill us yourself if you are strong enough. For as the man is, so is his strength."

Anger pumped adrenalin through Gideon's muscles. He had suffered enough because of those haughty kings. Humiliation before his soldiers could not be tolerated. Gideon singlehandedly killed the burly braggarts. He stripped their camels of the gaudy, costly ornaments and charms they wore as necklaces of the royal family. A herald of victory rolled across Israel. Gideon was a Nevertheless hero used by God to deliver Israel.

Rallies were held to persuade Gideon to become king over Israel. "You have delivered us from the Midianites. You deserve to become our ruler!" Israel reasoned. "You, your son, and your grandsons need to set up a dynasty of rulers of Israel," they pleaded.

Gideon refused, "Neither I nor my son will rule over you. The LORD shall rule over you. He is responsible for this victory over Midian. All I request of you is that each of you give me the gold earrings you took from the enemy." Israel had no such practice as wearing earrings, but their heathen enemy denoted their insulting curse to Isaac and his descendants and their allegiance to Baal by wearing icons of gold in their ears and adorning their camels with necklaces of such. Gideon desired to take those from the Israelites lest they be tempted with that heathen practice.

(The first account of the custom of a particular people wearing earrings is found in Genesis 21:9-21. Abraham had a son by a slave woman named Hagar. Ishmael was later caught mocking Abraham's legitimate son, Isaac, and was thrown out of the house with his mother. Sarah, Abraham's wife, said, "Ishmael shall not be heir with my son, Isaac." Although it had been her idea to have her husband sire a son by her personal slave, Sarah refused Ishmael equal rights or the right of inheritance as the first-born son because he mocked Isaac. God agreed with Sarah, so Abraham sent the boy and his mother away. Ishmael married an Egyptian because his mother was an Egyptian. Therefore, he began practicing the customs of Egypt. Slaves had their ears pierced and wore earrings to cover the piercing when they escaped or were freed. His descendants wore earrings to denote that they were Ishmaelite, honoring Ishmael because they taught that he had been unjustifiably disinherited by Abraham. That explains why the descendants hated the Israelites. The Midianites were also descendants of Abraham from Keturah, his wife after Sarah. Abraham also disinherited them. The Bible calls the two other women, with whom Abraham had children, concubines or illegitimate wives. He gave them gifts and sent them away from his son Isaac. Those boys also wore the sign of freed slaves, the earrings [Genesis 25:1-7; I Chronicles 1:32]. That was the identifying factor for Jacob's older sons when they sold their brother, Joseph, into slavery to the caravan of merchants going to Egypt [Genesis 37:25-28]. Since Israel had been delivered from slavery when

Nevertheless, God

God delivered them from Egypt, Gideon did not want Israel to renew the practice of looking like shamed freed slaves. He knew that the generation of Israelites who had crossed Jordan River to possess Canaan had not borne the shame of slavery as had their parents and grandparents, who had died in the wilderness. Israel had been freed, had declared the LORD as their God, and had taken on the practices of godliness. Therefore, Gideon asked for the earrings so he could melt them and recycle them as something else. Remember also that Aaron chose earrings to make the golden calf at Sinai shortly after Israel came out of Egypt and when Moses had gone to the top of Sinai to talk with God forty days. That explanation reveals why Aaron chose specifically to use earrings, which covered the holes that had been bored into their ears to show that they had been slaves to Egypt. Later, God gave this sanction to pierce the ear to denote that a Hebrew person had freely declared allegiance to his master for whom he desired to become a servant forever [Deuteronomy 15:17]. No free citizen of Israel had his or her ears pierced.)

"We gladly give them to you," the people replied. They spread a cloak on the ground, and each man removed the earrings from his loot and threw them on the heap Gideon had of ornaments, the collars, the purple garments from the Midianite kings, and chains that their camels had worn. They weighed the bundle of earrings, 1,700 shekels. That converts to roughly 266 modern-day pounds since a shekel weighed two and one-half ounces. Gideon melted those earrings and made an ephod from them. An ephod was a garment. Gideon made a garment of gold mail and displayed it as a trophy of victory in his hometown, Ophrah. It became a tourist attraction for Israel to admire but eventually became an object of worship. That created problems for Israel for years.

Chapter 6
Abimelech, the Usurping Judge

Because the Midianites were soundly defeated, Israel enjoyed quietness for forty years. Gideon lived in his own house and married many women. He had seventy sons. As if his many wives and sons did not satisfy Gideon, he had an extramarital affair with a woman in Shechem. With that concubine Gideon had another son, and they named him Abimelech. His name denoted that he was expected to produce a lineage of kings. Abimelech took his name seriously and plotted to live up to its meaning.

Abimelech was raised ostracized from the legal children Gideon had fathered. However, he had admired and wanted to emulate his father to the point that he desired to take Gideon's place and to become a ruler over Israel. Gideon enjoyed a long life but then died and was buried in Ophrah, leaving no designated heir to lead the family. Israel came to grieve the death of Gideon and left feeling abandoned of spiritual leadership. The void led Israel to lament Gideon's death. "He should have set up one of his sons to rule," they conjectured. "With Gideon gone, we have no connections to the Lord God. There is no need to worship God if we have no one to lead us in worship. No one can wear that gold armor as Gideon did," they reasoned. The people came often to view the ephod and to remember Gideon. Abimelech noted that and vowed to take advantage of the opportunity.

It was not long afterward that Israel's confusion and blaming turned her focus on another god, Baalim. Baalim was the ancient plurality of gods worshiped by the heathen nations who had settled in and had populated Canaan. Because Israel had not obeyed the LORD God JEHOVAH and since many of those heathen tribes still lived in Canaan, Israel again succumbed to the temptation of curiosity and lust. Shechem, the home of Gideon's illegitimate son, Abimelech, worshiped a god of Baalim called Baal–berith. That god was considered a covenant lord of Shechem.

Ironically, Shechem was where Jacob, the father of Israel, had entered into covenant promise with the LORD. Jacob had bought a parcel of land at Shechem and had made his home there. He had erected an altar to the LORD God JEHOVAH on his property, and his family worshiped at that altar (Genesis 33:18-20). After Jacob's sons murdered the entire population of the little town of Shechem in revenge for their sister's being sexually defiled, Jacob moved his family in fear that the neighbors would discover what had happened to Shechem and that they would launch an attack against him. Shechem had been abandoned but then had been repopulated by the Canaanites for many years. When Israel occupied the land nearly five hundred years after Jacob's sons had made the family flee, his descendants took the territory as part of the tribe of Ephraim. The Ephraimites had not driven out the Canaanites, and the heathen had become

Abimelech, the Usurping Judge

thorns pricking and gouging Israel's spiritual flesh and sides. When she desired to have a god like her neighbors, she began to worship the ephod Gideon had made. That led to further sin and to Israel's making a covenant to worship Baal–berith. Then, they forsook God altogether and sold themselves to idolatry. "Gideon is dead. So is his God," they lamented. "Thus, neither he nor his family have any authority over us!" Spiteful resentment toward Gideon's family poisoned the tribe of Ephraim. Fueled by Abimelech's personal vendetta, the rebellion spread into a combative struggle for power. Israel lost her security and peace in the feud among her own people.

Of Gideon's seventy-one sons, only three have their names listed in Scripture: Jether, the eldest; Abimelech, the illegitimate son; and the youngest, Jotham. Jether was among Gideon's three hundred men chosen by God to defeat the Midianites. Jether had loyally followed his father from the time the army had been mustered until the victory was completed. He had not been among the fearful nor among the incautious at the water test. Unwaveringly, Jether had endured the arduous hours of pursuit of the fleeing Midianite kings. But Jether had not been aggressive enough in his own confidence in God to slay those kings once they were captured. He lost his prospective status as a hero in Israel.

Abimelech evidently had been born after the Midianites had been defeated and Israel was enjoying forty years of quietness. Abimelech was vain, following the wiles of his maternal relatives. The young man knew that his father had refused Israel's request to be the king of

Nevertheless, God

Israel. He also remembered that Gideon had forbidden that right for any of his sons. However, Gideon from the grave could not control his egomaniacal son. Abimelech returned to his mother's kinfolk in great bitterness after Gideon's funeral and the ensuing estate settlement had shortchanged him. He took his maternal relatives into confidence and plotted to become king! His uncles, great-uncles, cousins, and his grandfather all joined in the coronation, "Long live King Abimelech! Abimelech is king!" The entire town rallied to the cause in support of Abimelech. "United under one or divided by seventy sons of Gideon? Which would be better? Gideon is dead, and his sons will rise up and quarrel over who inherits their father's position as ruler. Abimelech is one of us. He will preserve the prosperity and security for our families here at home. What would Gideon's other sons do for us? Nothing! That's what! Abimelech is our king!" they shouted.

    Shechem became the headquarters for organizing the kingdom. Abimelech continued to spread his insinuations and lies about his brothers with subtle accusations against their character. His rhetoric resonated with many in Israel whose hearts had already turned from God. He gathered much financial support from the idolatrous church treasury, as well as from freewill donations. The single contribution from the church of Baal–berith was seventy pieces of silver! That was enough for Abimelech to hire like-minded mobsters to fulfill his orders. "To secure the absolute authority of my administration, we must destroy our opponents. Our first duty is to preserve

Abimelech, the Usurping Judge

Shechem's heritage and to firmly establish Shechem as the seat of government in Israel," Abimelech advised. "Gird on your weapons. We are marching on Ophrah and will slay those who oppose my administration." It was but a short march to Ophrah, the home and burial place for Gideon and his ancestors. The tiny village was surprised. Gideon's sons were unsuspecting and unarmed. In mockery the brothers were forced to gather around the prominent stone that Gideon had used as an altar to the LORD. "Ha, ha," Abimelech sneered. "Our father heralded this stone as memorable to his calling to be leader of Israel. He then destroyed the altar to Baal and cut down his grove. We'll now see if this stone will defend Gideon's sons with fire from heaven as Gideon's story says." Without mercy, Abimelech murdered sixty-nine of his brothers on that stone. The blood washed over the stone and soaked the ground around it. However, Jotham, the youngest boy, slipped away unnoticed and escaped. He fled to the top of Mount Gerizim, from which he observed the evils of his half-brother, who proceeded from the stone on which the angel had sat and talked with Gideon to Gideon's oak tree near the winepress. Men gathered from Shechem and Millo to the plain at the pillar of oak in Shechem and crowned Abimelech king. Jotham was informed of the terrible deeds and thanked God He had helped him to escape to Mount Gerizim (Judges 9).

Gerizim was chosen by God and Moses to be the place for Joshua to hold Israel's first memorial service after crossing Jordan River to possess Canaan. Mount

Nevertheless, God

Gerizim was called the mount of blessing (Deuteronomy 27:12-26; Joshua 8:33-35). From her slopes, Joshua had read the blessings God would pour upon Israel if she obeyed His commandments. Across the valley stood an opposing peak, the mount of cursing, Mount Ebal. Jotham chose refuge in the mount of blessing. He desired to obey the Lord. But when he opened his mouth to chide Abimelech, he did not pronounce anything but curses upon his evil brother and those who endorsed him.

"Listen, you men of Shechem, that God may listen to you. The trees went to anoint a king over them. They asked the olive tree, 'Reign over us.' The olive tree refused. 'Why should I leave my fatness by which men honor God and man just so I would be promoted over the trees?' So the trees said to the fig tree, 'Come, rule over us.' But the fig tree replied, 'Should I forsake my sweetness and my good fruit to be promoted over the trees?' Then the trees went to the vine and said, 'Come, rule over us.' The vine answered, 'Should I leave my wine which cheers both God and man to be promoted over the trees?' Then all the trees approached the bramble. 'Bramble, come, reign over us.' The bramble responded, 'If in truth you anoint me king over you, come put your trust in my shadow. If not, let fire come out of the bramble and devour the cedars of Lebanon.' "

Jotham upbraided further, "Now, therefore, if you have done truly and sincerely in making Abimelech king and if you have dealt well with Jerubbaal and his house by doing unto him according to what we deserve, then rejoice in Abimelech. Let him rejoice in you.

Abimelech, the Usurping Judge

"My father fought for you. He risked his life far beyond the call of ordinary duty to deliver you from the Midianites. But now you have risen against my father's house and have killed his sons upon one stone. You made Abimelech king, my illegitimate brother, because he is kin to you. If you have truly and sincerely dealt with Jerubbaal and his house, then rejoice. But if not, let fire come out from Abimelech and devour the men of Shechem and the house of Millo, your sacred fortress. Let fire come out from the men of Shechem and from the house of Millo and devour Abimelech." Jotham ran from his hiding place because he feared his brother.

Jotham fled to Beer, the well which long before Israel had dug with their staffs and had sung, "Spring up, O well," until God had ushered forth water from the dry ground. For three years Jotham found refuge in the surrounding village of Beer.

Meanwhile, in Shechem, God sent an evil spirit between Abimelech and the men of the city. The leaders of Shechem became disgruntled and plotted mutiny. Treachery festered like a boil about to rupture. "Why was Abimelech so cruel to his own brothers? If he is so cold to destroy his own father's sons, will he not do the same to us if we cross him? He holds us guilty of killing those brothers when he and his relatives who aided him are guilty of murdering those innocent men." So they organized a plot to overthrow Abimelech. Spies were stationed in the tops of the mountains.

They chose Gaal, the son of Ebed, to lead them. Gaal's relatives and the band of conspirators turned to robbery to finance their cause. They robbed everyone who came by them. Then they went to Shechem into the fields and robbed the vineyards. They gathered and pressed the grapes to drink for a merry celebration. They went to the church of Baal–berith and worshiped, eating, drinking, and cursing Abimelech. Gaal was not an Israelite by blood. He was a Hivite, a descendant of Hamor, the founder of Shechem (Genesis 33:18-20; 34). Baal–berith had always been the god of the Hivites, the direct descendants of Ham and his grandson Nimrod.

Abimelech was told the news of the revolt. He had not expected such to happen because he had been king for only three short years, but he felt confident that he had been doing a splendid job as king, would continue to rule, and could suppress the rebellion. He hurried his return to Shechem to handle the matter. Zebul, the ruler of Shechem, remained loyal to Abimelech and secretly kept him abreast of the situation.

Gaal had sarcastically smirked, "Who is this Abimelech that we should serve him? Is he not the son of Jerubbaal and Zebul is his officer? Come, serve the men of Hamor the father of Shechem. Why should we serve Abimelech and his relatives? Would to God I ruled this people—I would oust Abimelech! I challenge Abimelech to increase his army and to come out fighting." Many men of Shechem accepted Gaal as their king and began to fortify their city to face the war that was imminent.

The news from Zebul infuriated Abimelech. He was advised that his friend would continue to support Abimelech from within Shechem as a mole. Zebul said,

Abimelech, the Usurping Judge

"Go out at night and lay an ambush against the city at dawn." Abimelech took the advice and positioned four parties of his men to hide in the fields, waiting for daybreak. At the crack of dawn, Gaal went to his post at the city's entrance gate. Abimelech was alert and watchful of the movements of his enemy, Gaal. He signaled his men to begin advancing toward the city.

Zebul also was up early that morning and had joined Gaal at the city gate. Shadows moving across the fields arrested Gaal's attention. "People are coming from the mountains! I wonder what that means?" he queried.

Zebul laughed, "Your eyes are deceiving you. You merely see the shadows of the mountains as if they were men."

Gaal blinked and refocused his vision, "There *are* people coming down by the middle of the land, and more are coming along the plains of Meonenim!"

Zebul chuckled again. "What were you saying when you cursed Abimelech and bragged that you should not serve him? Where is your mouth now? Are not those the people whom you despised? Go out and fight with them, Gaal. Muster your forces and fight," Zebul dared.

The two forces clashed in the field. Gaal's men were trounced, and some tried to reenter the city. Zebul had a group of supporters blocking the entrance so that the wounded men could not return. He ordered, "You who followed Gaal, take your leader and move out of town. We don't want you living here." Zebul forced them out the gates of the city. The citizens and the warriors who had followed Gaal made camp in the open

Nevertheless, God

field outside the city walls. They spent the night wondering what would happen to them and their new leader.

Abimelech had returned to his camp to await the report from Zebul. The message arrived in short order. "Gaal and his people have been forced out of Shechem. Consider what you must do, for they are camped in the surrounding fields."

Abimelech divided his soldiers into three divisions. They attacked the open refugee camp the next morning. Abimelech fought against the city all that day and killed everyone he found. Some of the citizens took refuge in the tower of the church to Baal–berith. They trusted that their god would stop Abimelech's merciless behavior. He had already beaten the city down and had sown it with salt, and thousands of corpses lay bloating in the sun. They watched Abimelech leave Shechem and climb Mount Zalmon.

Mistaken relief spread a bit of cheer and praise to Berith for deliverance from Abimelech's wrath. However, the relief was short-lived.

Abimelech had received word that a remnant of the people of Shechem had holed up in the tower. He and his men took axes and went to the mountain to cut down tree branches to carry back to the tower. Abimelech said, "As you see me do, hurry, and do the same." So the army cut down large branches and shouldered them down the mountain. They piled the branches around the tower and set it on fire. Flames leaped high up the structure. The tower sucked the fire and smoke like a chimney. About a thousand men and women died in their sacred tower.

Abimelech, the Usurping Judge

Abimelech was emboldened by his success at repelling the coup. His troops were bloodthirsty, so they swept across to the city of Thebez. It is not clear why Abimelech spilled his wrath on Thebez. He probably suspected that the twin to Shechem would rise in protest to the destruction of a sacred shrine to their god Baal–berith. Memory of his own wrath toward his father's house resembled such possibilities in the making. Anyway, Abimelech knew there was a similar sacred tower to Berith in Thebez. When the attack came, the families of Thebez fled to their tower and bolted the door. They climbed the stairs to the top, where they had built a large room in which they could assemble for worship. They felt safe waiting out the battle behind the bolted door of their sacred confine. At the base of the tower, warriors of Thebez gave Abimelech a good match in warfare. Abimelech fought hard and had finally made it to the door of the tower with the intent to torch the door and the tower.

A woman of Thebez had fled to the tower with her millstone in her arms. The large stone was a valuable possession for any household, and she certainly did not want to have it stolen or broken. At the top of the tower, the woman could see the intent of their enemy. She leaned out the window and took careful aim before dropping the stone.

Abimelech saw the woman and the stone too late to jump away from danger. The stone hit with a blow that dealt a deadly crack to his skull. "Help me!" Abimelech cried to his armor bearer. "My skull is broken! Take your sword and kill me so it can't be said that a

Nevertheless, God

woman slew me!" The young man plunged his sword through the writhing man. He quit twitching, and his body lay still, dead!

"Abimelech is dead!" The announcement abruptly ended the assault against the tower. Abimelech's army melted away as each man stole home in defeat.

The news reached Jotham at Beer. He said, "God has returned the wickedness of Abimelech and the men of Shechem upon their own heads for having killed my father's seventy sons." The usurping judge of Israel had reigned for approximately three years.

CHAPTER 7

TOLA, THE RED WORM JUDGE
JAIR, THE ENLIGHTENED JUDGE

The tribe of Issachar was landlocked on three sides. The Jordan River bordered for a few miles on the east. The tribe of Manasseh lay south, sandwiched between Issachar and the tribe of Ephraim. For some unexplained reason, Tola, a man from Issachar, left his tribal state and moved south to Ephraim. The meaning of the name, Tola, may be the answer for his reason to have moved. *Tola* means "red worm." The humiliation of being constantly referred to as Red Worm seems also to reflect on his father, Puah, whose name meant "glitz and brilliance." Puah must have been a tinsel man who loved the limelight. Because the grandfather, Dodo, had an unusual name which meant "loving, doting," it is assumed that conflict arose in the family. By those three names depicting what each parent thought of his son, we gain a description of the conflict of personalities and ambitions amid three generations of Issachar's descendants.

Regardless of the circumstances, Tola had made his home in the town of Shamir in Mount Ephraim. The name *Shamir* means "thorns." The name denotes that Shamir had a natural defensive barrier around it. No human or animal enjoyed fighting through brambles and thorns to get to a destination, assuring Shamir relative safety. In that atmosphere Tola was chosen by God to be judge of Israel. His was a peaceful rule, and nothing exceptional seemed to have ruffled Israel's tranquility for the twenty-three years Tola was judge. Tola proved that God can use those who are belittled and maybe even ostracized if they remain true to God. He can make them bloom in another location among those not of their family, even if that location is surrounded by thorns.

The eighth judge of Israel was named Jair, who lived east of Jordan River in the land of Gilead, a mountainous region of Israel. The name *Jair* means "enlightened." Jair, like Tola, is given only a brief notation in the Scripture about his twenty-two years as judge of Israel. Times of peace seemed to have given the historians little subject matter about which to write. It is noted that Jair was a very industrious father of thirty sons. He was a prosperous man to have been able to provide each of his sons a donkey to ride. Those boys were taught how to grow their wealth and to hold it. The Bible states that each boy had his own city. Jair had invested in his sons the quality of leadership and financial management so that the memory of Jair was written in history that his contribution to Israel was his thirty sons, who ruled thirty cities under their father's administration, without ever having unrest, spiritual infidelity, or a breach of security. That alone is a powerful testimony. The descendants of Jair retained their integrity and leadership skills such that, years later, King David chose a chief leader from them (II Samuel 20:26).

Tola . . . Jair

First Chronicles 2:18-22 gives the genealogy of Jair. He was a descendant of Hezron, the father of Caleb. Caleb had been one of Israel's spies under Moses' leadership. At age sixty, Hezron fathered a son and named him Segub. Segub was then the father of Jair. Scripture states Caleb's age as eighty-five when he asked for his inheritance in Canaan west of Jordan River. Hezron's son Segub married into the tribe of Ephraim and settled east of the Jordan River in the territory Israel won from the kings, Sihon and Og. Jair ruled Israel within the first one hundred or so years after Israel had conquered the kingdoms of those heathen kings, Sihon and Og. His cousin, Othniel, also was a judge over Israel on the western side of Jordan River. They possibly were contemporaries (Judges 3:9; 10:3-5). It is possible that Jair's father, as a young person, had been at Sinai when God gave Moses the law and the Ten Commandments. Jair would have had an immediate example of godliness so he knew how to obtain peace from God for his people.

Chapter 8

JEPHTHAH, THE BANISHED JUDGE, RETURNED

After Tola and Zair were lost in the annals of history, Israel returned to her age-old pattern of rebellion against God. Her evil behavior corrupted her in the sight of God. Israel began to serve Baalim, the plurality of gods known as Baal and his wife, Ashtoreth. Those heathen gods of Syria, Zidon, Moab, Ammon, and the Philistines who lived among and around Israel wooed Israel's affection. Israel forsook the LORD and worshiped and served the heathen gods. In hot vexation, God sold Israel to the Philistines and Ammon. The Philistines occupied the Gaza strip along the Mediterranean Sea. Israel should have long before conquered the Philistines and destroyed her nation, but she had not done so. The Philistines partnered with Ammon to launch war against Israel. Ammon's territory was east of the Jordan River and was off-limits to Israel in her conquest of her promised land. God had forbidden Israel to go to war against Ammon because Ammon had possessed the inheritance of Lot, Israel's cousin and Abraham's nephew. However, Ammon lost her respect for that restriction from God (Deuteronomy 2:19, 37). Ammon had in his family history the lineage of Abraham's God. Abraham had taken Lot into his home after Lot's father had died. Lot had been nurtured by Abraham for years. Lot had gotten wealthy while living with Abraham but had split company and settled in the city of Sodom. Sodom and her twin city were torched by God while Lot escaped by the skin of his teeth because of Abraham's intercession with God. Lot lost his family in that rain of fire and brimstone. He eventually fled to a mountain and lived in a cave with his only survivors, his two daughters. Those daughters got their father drunk and forced Lot to father children with them. Ammon and Moab were those children born of incest. That severance from Abraham planted a corrupted knowledge of God in Ammon so that evil severed the sacred bonds to the LORD of Abraham. Ammon had become an idolatrous nation that in turn hated Israel (Genesis 11:27-31; 19).

Israel quickly was swallowed by her allure to Baalim and Ashtoreth. The malpractice of her religious leaders maligned the LORD God of Israel. The cancer spread across the Jordan River, rapidly spreading religious malignancy to vex all Israel east and west of the Jordan. The Ammonites in fearless abandon made life miserable for Israel because of it. Ammon waged war against Gilead east of Jordan and with the tribes of Judah, Benjamin, and Ephraim to the west of Jordan. With Ammon invading from the east and the Philistines at war with the tribes on the western flanks, on the Mediterranean seaboard, Israel was in sore straits. She was caught between two powerful forces that greatly desired to wipe Israel out. Israel cried to the LORD, "We have sinned

Jephthah, the Banished Judge, Returned

against You. We have forsaken our God. We have served Baalim" (Judges 10:10).

The LORD said, "Did I not deliver you from the Egyptians, the Amorites, from Ammon, the Philistines, the Zidonians, the Amalekites, and the Maonites who oppressed you? You cried to Me then and I delivered you, yet you have forsaken Me and served other gods. I will not deliver you any more. Go, cry to the gods you have chosen. Let them deliver you in the time of your tribulation" (Judges 10:11-14).

The Egyptians had enslaved Israel in Egypt for four hundred years. The other mentioned enemies of Israel lived in or near Canaan; the Amorites were mountaineers who descended from Ham, Noah's son. The Philistines were wanderers who also descended from Ham and lived along the seacoast of the Mediterranean Sea. The Zidonians were fishermen and were seafaring people who also lived near the coast. The Amalekites descended from Esau and lived south of Canaan. They were a warlike people who had inherited Esau's fierce temperament and hatred for Esau's twin brother, Jacob, known as Israel. The Maonites were local heathen inhabitants who had not been driven out of Canaan by Israel in her conquest of the Promised Land.

When God chided Israel for her sin, Israel cried more earnestly, "We have sinned. Do to us whatever You think seems good to You; only deliver us! We beg You this day." Israel arose from prayer and cleaned house. She put away the strange heathen gods and returned to serving the LORD. Repentance brought turning from evil

Nevertheless, God

and moving toward God. His soul was grieved for the misery of Israel.

To compound matters further, the Ammonites had pitched camp against Israel in Gilead east of the Jordan River. The family of Gilead had been mighty warriors, who had been very successful in securing territory for Israel. In honor and respect for Gilead, a large portion of the tribe of Gad was named after him (Joshua 12:2-5). When Ammon mustered against Israel, Israel called a council of war held at Mizpeh of Gilead (Judges 10:17). Mizpeh was so named by Jacob as the place where he and Laban, his father-in-law, had signed a peace agreement hundreds of years before. Mizpeh had originally been spelled Mizpah, before the conquest by Israel (Genesis 31:42-52).

The Ammonites insisted on war or, as an alternative, Israel was to turn over the deed to all her land from the Arnon River to the Jabbok River to the Jordan River. That basically was the territory Israel had fought for and had won from two Amorite kings, Sihon and Og, before Moses had died. That was about one-third of the territory in which Israel had settled east of Jordan. Gilead was in the mountainous area of the tribe of Gad. Gilead suffered the most from the plundering of the Ammonites. The Gileadites were in jeopardy of losing their homeland. The people and princes of Gilead held a think tank at Mizpeh and inquired among themselves for a qualified military leader for Israel's defense. No one present was brave enough to head or capable of leading an untrained, newly assembled militia. Finally, someone recalled that

Jephthah, the Banished Judge, Returned

their exiled brother, Gilead's illegitimate son, was a man of valor. "We need someone like Jephthah," they said.

"But we don't like Jephthah. He is the son of a scarlet woman. We ran him off, remember? We all had agreed to disinherit him."

"Yeah, we remember. You had said, 'Leave, or we will take strong measures to plant your carcass where the wild beasts and birds will pick your bones.' Then you chased him out of the house with a sword. We remember that Jephthah mounted his horse and kicked his flanks. As he galloped away, the dust boiled as angrily as did your fury. Jephthah could have bested your swordsmanship easily, but he had refused to fight family."

"Send for Jephthah," another man urged. "Where is he now?"

"He has moved to the land of Tob. We've learned that he has assembled quite a group of such men as he, capable men of war," one of the brothers suggested. "Of all the sons of Gilead, none compare to the might and valor of Jephthah."

So the men of Gilead sent messengers north to the land of Tob. They did not ask but rather ordered Jephthah, "Come, and be our captain so that we can fight the Ammonites." Those men had been very short- and mean-tempered with Jephthah when their family inheritance had been given. They had forced Jephthah out of his proper inheritance because he had been born to a harlot mother. Those legitimate sons were haughty and talked fierce but in reality were wimps when it came to being real leaders in war.

Jephthah replied, "Didn't you hate me and expel me from my father's house? Why do you come to me now when you are in distress?"

"Because you are our brother. We have come to ask you to become head over us as our captain to lead us in war against Ammon."

Jephthah pressed the issue. "If you take me home again to fight Ammon and the LORD gives me the victory, will you declare that I am head of the family?"

"Yes, we will. The LORD be witness between us if we do not do as you say," they agreed in desperation.

The household of Jephthah and his band of men packed their belongings and moved south to Mizpeh, the place of the watchtower of witness stones. He and his band of warriors organized the relatives of Gilead. While the men were training to do battle, Jephthah made some inquiries to stall any attack Ammon had planned. Messengers took the inquiries to the king of Ammon. "What are you doing? Why do you attack Israel in our land?"

The haughty, presumptuous king sent back the reply, "Israel took away my land when she came up from Egypt. Restore me that land bordered by the rivers of Arnon, Jabbok, and Jordan, and there will be no need for me to fight."

Jephthah knew the history of his people. He had names, dates, and times of historical events, for Moses and Joshua had recorded them and had preserved the records in the archives of Israel. He sent back the messengers with the facts of history that dispelled the fallacy of Ammon (Judges 11:15-27). "The history books prove that your claims are fallacious. Israel did not take your land and has never invaded your territory. In fact, Israel never invaded your brother Moab's land either. Israel walked through the wilderness to the Red Sea, then to Kadesh. At Kadesh, Israel sent messengers to the king of Edom requesting passage through the land of Edom, but he refused. Then Israel requested passage through the land of Moab and was refused. So Israel stayed at Kadesh for a while before going around both Edom and Moab through the wilderness. Israel camped on the other side of Arnon on the opposite side of Moab's border. She didn't enter the border of Moab because the LORD our God forbade Israel to trespass on your inheritance.

"Israel sent messages to Sihon, king of the Amorites, requesting passage through his land. He gathered his army at Jahaz and attacked Israel. The LORD God of Israel delivered Sihon and all his people into Israel's hand. Israel smote the Amorites and possessed their land from Arnon to Jabbok and from the wilderness to the Jordan River. It was our God who dispossessed the Amorites. Should you now possess that land? Why don't you possess that which your god, Chemosh, gives you? Whomever the LORD our God drives out from before Israel, we will possess that land," Jephthah declared.

He went on to relate more of the story. "Are you any better than Balak the son of Zippor, king of Moab? Did he ever strive against Israel? Did he ever fight against Israel while we dwelt in Heshbon, Aroer, and all those towns and cities that lay along the coast of Arnon for the past three hundred years? If that land belonged to

Nevertheless, God

you, why have you not repossessed it during those three hundred years since Israel took possession of it? I have not sinned against you, but you do me wrong to fight me. The LORD, the Judge, will judge between Ammon and Israel," Jephthah retorted.

The history lesson was too much for the king of Ammon. His own version of history had rewritten the account in favor of his own people. He could not lose face before his people to whom he had taught his twisted version. "War! Death to Israel!" he swore. "Ammon will not be made out a liar. We shall march to the battle."

Jephthah quickly mustered his men to march to battle as well. The Spirit of the LORD came upon Jephthah. He rallied his men, and they left their homes in Mizpeh of Gilead and went to meet Ammon. As they went, Jephthah vowed to God, "If You shall without fail deliver Ammon into my hands, then when I return to my house, I will offer up to the LORD as a burnt offering whatever comes first from my door to meet me when I return in peace from this battle" (Judges 11:30-31).

The troops met in a mighty clash of swords and spears. God gave Jephthah a decisive victory. Ammon's soldiers were slain even as they fled. From Aroer to Minnith through twenty cities, then to the plains and the vineyards, a very great slaughter of Ammonite troops lay strewn over acres of battleground. Jephthah marched his men home in triumph.

From a distance Jephthah could see his new home decorated for festivities. A large welcome party had gathered to celebrate victory. His young daughter had

Jephthah, the Banished Judge, Returned

prepared much of the gaieties because she was so proud of her father's courage and bravery. Jephthah stood a little taller with his home in view. His weary shoulders straightened in a march of triumph up the hill. He kept his eyes on the front door of his home as he called a greeting, "Hey, I'm home!"

He wondered that there were no chickens scurrying about to greet him, nor did any lambs bound across the pasture from the barn to bleat for a scratching. Not even the sheepdog had pounced on him with a friendly, wagging tail and syrupy tongue. Instead, the door burst open with a greeting, "Surprise! Now, let the party begin!" Out danced his only child with her arms flung open wide to hug her champion dad. Behind her came the entire welcoming committee, dancing to the beat of tambourines. Jephthah's broad smile and pleasure of the reception abruptly turned into sorrowful tears. Not even the fact of his victory over Ammon could replace the happiness that the sight had robbed from him. With a heart-wrenching wail, Jephthah tore his garment and fell to his knees in grief.

"What is wrong, Father?" his daughter asked. "We heard news that you are now head of the entire family of Gilead because of your victory over Ammon. Has something terrible happened that we haven't heard? Are you injured? Do you not like the welcoming festivities I planned? Please, tell me, my dear, hero father."

Through wracking sobs, Jephthah choked out his grief, "It is nothing that you assume, my dearest child. It is you that brought such grief to me!"

"I'm so sorry, Father. I do not understand. What have I done?"

Jephthah continued holding his sobbing daughter tightly against his shoulder. "You have brought me very low. You trouble me because I opened my mouth with a vow to the Lord. I cannot change my vow."

"By all means, if you have vowed to the Lord, do as you have vowed. How can I keep you from fulfilling such a vow?"

"It was a rash vow, and it pains me deeply to tell you. But I vowed to offer to the Lord as a burnt sacrifice whatever first came out my door to greet me when I returned in victory," he sobbed. "I cannot break a vow to the Lord. I am so very sorry. I am truly a broken, defeated man though I did get victory over Ammon."

The brave girl straightened her shoulders and released her hug. She blew her nose on her handkerchief and dried her tears. "Come, Father. Do as you have vowed. I submit because the Lord has given you vengeance against Ammon." She paused, then spoke again, "I ask permission that I might first go alone with my friends to hike upon the mountains, where we can enjoy the beauties of the mountains of Gilead for a couple of months and have some fun and relaxation before you do what you have to do to me. There I will be free to cry or laugh without breaking your heart."

"You are a most unusual child, my dear. Of course you may go, and if you can have any peace and enjoyment with such a sentence from this broken, wounded father, I would never forbid it." The girls packed their

Jephthah, the Banished Judge, Returned

hiking gear, their sleeping bags, the trail mixes, jerky, and canteens, then sadly snaked over the mountain behind the house. The household was cheerless and lonely without the sparkle of the girl's exuberant personality.

Mrs. Jephthah wept frequently for her child, "She shall never know the joy of having a family of her own. She shall never give us those wonderful grandchildren to spoil. She will never be able again to have parties with her friends and bring wildflowers to my table. How on earth can I bear it?" Jephthah could do nothing but hold his tongue and swallow his own pain with large helpings of self-flagellations for being so rash in his zeal to receive assurance from the LORD of a victory which had been already promised by the LORD. God had made the promise long before to defend Israel when she repented and turned to Him. Jephthah should have also read that in the writings of history from which he so accurately wrote his enemy.

At the sight of the girls snaking their way back over the mountain toward home, Jephthah hardly knew how to respond. The Bible is not clear exactly what he did with the girl, but it is believed that he shut her away as he would do a lamb for purification before taking it to be offered as a sacrifice. If that is true, his daughter may have been taken to Shiloh to the Tabernacle to live dedicated wholly to God, similar to the vow Hannah made to God about her son Samuel some years later (I Samuel 1:11-28). This probably is what happened because the LORD forbade human sacrifices being burnt upon an altar (Deuteronomy 12:30-31). Whatever the case, each year thereafter, the girl's friends would revisit their hiking trails for four days to talk about their friend, the daughter of Jephthah.

Nothing seemed to go very well for Jephthah after he gave his daughter away. Soon thereafter, the men of Ephraim traveled north to visit Jephthah. They had a severe grievance over the war with Ammon. "Why did you not call us to help fight the Ammonites?" they fumed. "We are so angry that we intend to burn your house down with you in it. You are merely fugitives of Ephraim and Manasseh, a bunch of illegitimate rogues" (Judges 11:3; 12:4).

Jephthah was dazed by their audacity. "I and my people were at great strife with Ammon. I called for you to help, but you would not deliver us. So I took my life in my hands, and my men and I went over and fought Ammon ourselves. The LORD delivered Ammon into my hand. Why are you then coming to fight me, seeing that the LORD gave the victory?" Jephthah blew his bugle to muster his men immediately. The Ephraimites were held at bay until warriors assembled.

Ephraim would not surrender or concede defeat until the men of Gilead took arms and killed forty-two thousand warriors of Ephraim. A part of the slaughter took place at the ferry crossings of the Jordan River. Since the Gileadites spoke a different dialect than did the Ephraimites, the passengers boarding the ferries were asked to say the password, Shibboleth. If they could only say, "Sibboleth," they identified themselves as fleeing Ephraimites and thus became candidates for the sword.

Jephthah, the Banished Judge, Returned

Jephthah judged Israel for six years. He died and was buried in an unspecified city of Gilead. He never really got to enjoy his acclaim as mighty captain or as head of the Gilead family. It seems that Jephthah's rash vow had crushed his zest for living, and he never had any more children to revive that relish of life.

As an informative bit of biblical history, the story of Jephthah took place about sixty-six years before Israel demanded a king and Samuel anointed Saul the son of Kish of the tribe of Benjamin to be king.

To arrive at that date the years of Judges 11:26 and I Kings 6:1 are used.

```
  480 years Temple started after Exodus from Egypt
-  300 years after Sihon and Og when Jephthah began to judge
-   40 years Israel wandered in the wilderness (Numbers 14:33)
-   30 years Eli's judgeship (1 Samuel 4:18) (40 years less 10
              years overlap with Jephthah)
   110 years between Eli and the Temple
-   40 years for David's reign as kings of Israel
-    4 years Solomon had reigned when starting to build Temple
    66 years between Eli and King David
-   20 years Samuel judged alone
-    6 years for Jephthah's rule before Eli
    40 years approximate for Saul to reign king of Israel
```

During the sixty-six years between Eli and David, Samuel was the single judge of Israel for about twenty years after Eli died. The news of the capture of the ark of God had caused Eli to fall backward off a wall and to break his neck. Eli's sons were dead. His sons, Hophni and Phinehas, had died when the Philistines captured the ark they had carried into battle. Samuel's sons became of age. The ark of God had remained displaced from the Tabernacle in Shiloh for twenty years. It had been returned from captivity by the Philistines, who had kept it seven months, but the ark had been taken to Kirjath-jearim to Abinadab's house (I Samuel 7:1-2). Samuel did not have it returned to Shiloh. He was not authorized to handle the ark because only direct descendants of Aaron could do that. Although Samuel was a Levite, a priest, and a judge, he could not enter the Holiest of Holies where the ark was supposed to reside. Eli and his sons died the day the ark was captured, and Eli's grandson was born that same day. The direct descendants of Aaron were too young to fill the position of high priest. This explains why the ark was displaced many years (I Samuel 4:19-21; 14:2-3; 22:9). It appears that Ahitub, Ichabod's brother, actually became the high priest and his son after him, yet Ahitub did not become of age until Samuel was the judge of Israel for many years.

First Samuel 12:11 names several judges whom Samuel called to memory as he chided Israel for rejecting the rule of God's judges for a king: Jerubbaal or Gideon, Bedan, Jephthah, then Samuel. Bedan is believed to be the same as Abdon in Judges 12:13-15 because all those, including Samuel, had judged Israel from tribes east of Jordan. Mizpeh, east of Jordan, had been a common denominator among several judges, including Samuel. Hebrews 11:32 also names Gideon, Barak, Samson, Jephthah, then Samuel in the list of those who by

Jephthah, the Banished Judge, Returned

faith had subdued the enemies of God. Because of these two confirmations of Scripture, the reasonable conclusion is that Samuel knew Jephthah to have been a contemporary with Eli when Eli became a judge at age fifty-eight and died at ninety-eight (I Samuel 4:15, 18). Samuel had served as a young priest with Eli in the Tabernacle at Shiloh from the time Samuel was a young boy. Samuel was raised by Eli in the Tabernacle and learned much of the historical facts from Eli. The Tabernacle, after all, had housed the sacred writings and records of Israel's history since Moses had placed the law of the LORD there. Samuel would have had access to those manuscripts since he lived with Eli for many years. Samuel was well versed in the Word of the LORD (I Samuel 3:19-21). Scripture does not state when Samuel married nor when he moved to Ramah (I Samuel 2:11; 7:15-17), but he did become a circuit judge stationed in Ramah.

Because Samuel's grown sons became greedy for money, Israel demanded a king. After twenty years of ruling faithfully, Samuel consulted God about the matter. That was when God instructed Samuel to anoint Saul of Gibeah king. The ark remained at Kirjath–jearim and in Gibeah during Samuel's judgeship and through King Saul's reign of forty years (I Samuel 10:26; 14:16-19). Therefore, the ark would have been displaced for approximately sixty years from the Tabernacle of Moses before David became king and approximately ten more years until David moved to Jerusalem and had built a tabernacle for the ark and set in order the Levites for musicians, singers, porters, and such for continual worship and praise to God. In the meantime, the Tabernacle that Moses had built had been moved from Shiloh to Nob and from Nob to Gibeon, under Saul's rule as king. The original brazen altar also remained with Moses' Tabernacle (I Samuel 21:1-6; II Chronicles 1:3-6). However, the sacred ark had not made those moves.

These reasons could explain why Scripture listed the names of Samson, Jephthah, then Samuel in succession because they were briefly contemporaries with Eli, some in the early years of his life and into his priesthood and some in the later years, for Eli lived to be ninety-eight years old. Samson and Jephthah were the last of the major warrior judges who actually delivered Israel while numerous other judges ruled during times of peace. Eli judged Israel forty years. Those forty years were contemporary years with all the judges of Israel from Jephthah to Samuel with some overlapping their terms as judges with Samson, who judged Israel twenty years toward the latter years of Eli's priesthood.

Philistine dominance had begun to vex Israel little by little for years until Israel was overwhelmed (Judges 10:6-18). That was simultaneous with Jephthah's war with Ammon before Judges 13:1 introduced Samson into a time when Israel was enslaved by the Philistines.

When the Philistines captured the ark of the LORD, this act brought earthquakes in the spirit realm, which caused Israel to question national security under the leadership of judges and priests twenty years after the death of Eli. Ironically enough, Saul, the first king of Israel, did not seem too concerned that the ark was dis-

Jephthah, the Banished Judge, Returned

placed from the Tabernacle. He even blocked access to the ark for David (I Chronicles 13:3). When David became king, he returned the ark to a central place for national access in worship. King David had the ark taken to Jerusalem (II Samuel 6:1-17). It was placed in a tabernacle made for worship and praise until David's son Solomon built the Temple and placed the ark permanently there.

CHAPTER 9

IBZAN, ELON, AND ABDON: THREE ORDINARY MEN WHO JUDGED ISRAEL

After Jephthah, a man of Bethlehem named Ibzan judged Israel for seven years. Nothing remarkable was recorded about his leadership except that he too must have been a good father. He excelled in producing children of esteem. It is recorded that Ibzan had thirty sons and thirty daughters. With so many children for whom to find spouses, he was kept busy planning and implementing weddings for his offspring. He took from abroad thirty women for his sons to marry and sent his thirty daughters abroad to marry. After the weddings were over, the parting entry to the history book is that Ibzan died and was buried in Bethlehem, his home.

After Ibzan a judge from the tribe of Zebulun ruled. His name was Elon, and he judged Israel for ten years. Nothing else is said about his administration. It can be assumed that his was a time of peace for Israel as were the previous seven years under Ibzan's authority. Elon died and was buried in Aijalon of Zebulun. Aijalon was the place where Joshua had commanded the moon to stand still. A large valley stretched across the border between the tribes of Dan and Ephraim. That was the valley of Aijalon (Joshua 10:12).

Nevertheless, God

After Elon, there arose a judge named Abdon, the son of Hillel, a Pirathonite, who judged Israel for eight years. Abdon produced forty sons and provided fine mounts for his sons to ride. There was a flourishing family among his siblings as well, for he had thirty nephews. The family had to have abundant prosperity for Abdon to provide fine mounts for those boys also. It would seem that they had a horse ranch with many stables and large acreage on which they could ride. Those seventy horsemen riding on equally fine mounts would have presented a spectacular viewing. When Abdon died, he was buried in Pirathon of Ephraim, in the mount of the Amalekites. Thus ended twenty-five years of relatively uneventful years of peace for Israel under three judges who had ruled from different parts of Israel west of Jordan River. They likely ruled during Eli's lifetime. First Chronicles 8:30-33 and 9:36-39 gives the genealogy of Abdon to be the brother to Kish, who was the father of King Saul, Israel's first king.

Chapter 10
Samson, the Weak Superman

The following story reveals that neither godly parents nor righteous teaching, family holiness, or personal miracles will suffice if a stubborn, lustful heart will not live for God. This story happened in a time when evil had again eaten like a cancer into Israel's relationship with God. Consequently, the Philistines were allowed to dominate Israel for forty years (Judges 13:1). Forty years is a lifetime for many people. Within four decades a whole generation could have been so warped and polluted with ungodliness that the cause for God seemed dead. Those forty years seemed to coincide with Jephthah and beyond, for King Saul also fought the Philistines. Also, David as a young teenager killed their champion, Goliath. Therefore, it is reasoned that those forty years of Philistine domination lasted from the time of Eli's judgeship until Philistine dominance was broken by David's killing Goliath. From that time, the Philistines challenged Israel in war but never again gained supremacy over Israel even when they killed King Saul. During that period of time before Saul, Samson judged Israel for twenty years. Samson ruled on the west side of Jordan River while Jephthah judged on the east side.

The story began with a farmer named Manoah and his wife. They worked their little farm in Zorah of the

Nevertheless, God

tribe of Dan. They had not forgotten the LORD. Judges 13-16 records the historical account of that family and the so-called superman of the Bible. Mrs. Manoah sometimes went to the field alone to work while her husband did other things. As was the custom of that day, women who could not bear children were often considered to be almost worthless or subservient to their husbands. It may have been that she had the disapproval of her husband so much that he treated her as a servant and made her work in the field alone. This may be the reason her given name is not recorded in the account. Regardless, the woman was alone one day, sweating over her chores. That she was a good woman and a praying woman is evident in the occurrence that happened that day.

An unidentifiable man appeared to the woman as she worked. He suddenly became visible to the woman without her knowing where or how he had found her. Of course, the woman was frightened by the terrible-looking stranger. The sight rooted her feet in the dirt so that she could neither flee nor speak. The stranger spoke the only words by which the woman could receive comfort at the time. "Behold, you have no children because you are barren and cannot bear children, but you shall conceive and bear a son." The woman gasped at the prospect. She listened as the man continued, "Now, therefore, beware and do not drink wine nor strong drink and eat nothing unclean. For you shall conceive and bear a son who is never to have a razor come upon his head. He shall be a Nazarite unto God from the womb. He shall begin to deliver Israel from the hands of the Philistines." Note:

Samson, the Weak Superman

Samson began his divine command but never completed the job of deliverance from the Philistines' stranglehold on Israel.

When the awe-producing stranger vanished, the woman ran home breathless. "Manoah, Manoah!" she cried. "A man of God came to me in the field. He looked like an angel of God, very terrible. I didn't ask where he came from nor his name, but he told me that I shall conceive and bear a son. I am not to drink wine nor strong drink nor eat any unclean thing, for the boy is to be a Nazarite to God from the womb until he dies." She failed to report that her son was destined by the call of God to deliver Israel from the Philistines. Maybe that point was insignificant in the priorities of her yearning for a child.

Manoah sensed the sincerity of his wife's report. However, he could hardly believe that God would prefer to reveal such a miracle to his wife without having consulted him, the husband, first. He had to see the angel for himself and to ask a few questions of his own. So he prayed, "O my Lord, let the man of God which you did send come again unto us and teach us what we shall do to the child that shall be born." He believed that if his wife had really seen such a being, she would have been toast (Judges 13:22). What a rebuking surprise when the terrible one did return!

Manoah's wife sat alone again in the field when the man appeared. Quickly she ran to her husband. "The man has returned! He is the same man who came to me the other day. He is in the field!"

With some trepidation Manoah followed his wife

Nevertheless, God

to the field. Noting that he did not rush ahead of her speaks of his hesitance to validate her claim. His reluctance spoke of doubt that such an experience could have been reality. The fact that he followed her makes his prayer appear as audacious sarcasm. But to save face and to prove the sincerity of his unbelief, he shadowed his wife to the field, not really expecting the terrible one to be there. Indeed, he was there, waiting! "Ar-r-r-re you the man who spoke to my wife?" Manoah sputtered.

"I am," the man replied.

"Well, then, let your words come to pass," answered Manoah. "Tell us how we shall raise the child, and what shall be his purpose and assignment in life?"

The angel repeated the instructions he had given to the woman. "Of all I have said to the woman, let her beware. She may not eat any fruit from a vine nor drink wine nor strong drink. She is to eat nothing unclean: All that I commanded her, let her observe."

Manoah suddenly desired to test the genuineness of the man. He still did not perceive that he was an angel of the LORD. "I pray that you will let us detain you until we have cooked some veal for you," Manoah suggested.

The angel answered, "Though you detain me, I will not eat your food. And if you do offer a burnt offering, it must be offered unto the LORD." He knew that Manoah did not yet believe him to be an angel.

Manoah pressed, "What's your name so that when your words do come to pass, we may do you honor?"

The response was very much like the response Jacob had received many years before when he wrestled all night with such a being and had gotten both a name change and a crippled hip (Genesis 32:24-29). "Why do you ask for my name, seeing it is a secret?" the angel questioned (Judges 13:18).

So Manoah did take food and a kid and offered it to the LORD upon a rock. The angel did wonders, and as the flames devoured the offering, he ascended in the tongue of fire and was seen no more. Manoah and his wife saw it and fell facedown in the dirt.

"What being have we just seen?" Manoah exclaimed, his knees knocking and his eyes bulging in fear. "We shall surely die, for we have seen God!"

His wife had a calmer and clearer perception of the angel. She boldly declared, "If the LORD would have desired to kill us, He would not have received the burnt offering or the meat offering from us. He would not have shown us such things, nor would He have told us such things as He did." She believed, for she had seen the angel twice and lived.

Manoah shook his head, and the couple staggered home in awe. As the angel had foretold, they did have a son. She named him Samson, meaning "like the sun; awe inspiring." The name reflected her first impression of the angel's appearance and of his words to her in the field. The child grew, and the LORD blessed him.

After a time, Samson began to be moved by the Spirit of the LORD as he traveled from Zorah, his birthplace, to the Camp of Dan to Eshtaol, a town in Judah. Zorah was situated at the southeast tip of the territory of Dan, and the Camp of Dan was the name of a place in

Nevertheless, God

Kirjath–jearim in the tribe of Judah, where some families of Dan from Zorah and Eshtaol had set up a military camp (Judges 18:11-12). Six hundred men with weapons of war were stationed in that camp. They called their camp "Mahaneh–dan." The camp was near the town of Hebron, and Samson may have visited relatives there. He was recognized as having a call of God upon him. Then, as an adult, he ventured beyond Israel's borders to see the camp of the Philistines, and trouble began.

Samson evidently desired to see for himself the enemy's style of life and the lay of their land. He visited the Philistine city of Timnath, a town located inside the tribe of Dan, which had been repossessed and occupied by the Philistines for years. Satan focused on Samson's weakness, his lust for the love of a woman. In the territory of Baal worshipers who specialized in lewd sensuality, Samson succumbed to the spirit of the town. He saw a pretty Philistine woman and longed to marry her.

In the custom of that day, parents arranged marriages for their children. It was not considered necessary for the prospective bride and groom to know each other before their engagement. However, it was considered absolutely essential that the parents approved the match. Samson somewhat overrode the protocol for the custom after he saw the Philistine woman. Upon his arrival at home, he demanded his father, "I have seen a Philistine woman in Timnath whom I want to marry. Now, therefore, get her for me."

The disrespectful demand was rebuffed by his father. "Is there never a woman among our kin or among all our people that you choose a wife from the uncircumcised Philistines?"

Samson retorted, "Father, get her for me, for she pleases me well." Samson not only held determined disregard for custom, but he also reproached the command of God not to intermarry with the heathen of Canaan. He did not value the Abrahamic covenant over his immediate, lustful desires. From that time, Samson became well known for touting his brute strength as a means to attract heathen women. However, Samson's obstinate choice did not negate God's call and purpose for his life. God used that arrogance to thrust Samson into the divine mission for which he was born.

Manoah, his wife, and their son prepared to go to Timnath. For an Israelite family to cross the boundary of their dominating governmental power must have taken them through rigorous experiences that made it difficult to proceed. Nonetheless, Samson rushed ahead of his parents and cut through the vineyards of Timnath to shorten his route. During the delay, a young lion roared and leaped out to attack Samson. He caught the lion with his bare hands, and the Spirit of the LORD empowered him to rip that lion apart. He threw the carcass aside and proceeded to his prospective bride's home. He did not tell anyone about the lion. The stardust of love swamped his mind with lustful desire. His parents arrived at the girl's father's home, and the bargaining began.

The Manoah family left the girl with her parents, and they returned to Zorah with the wedding contract sealed. Samson went home to prepare for the event while

Nevertheless, God

his woman friend did the same in Timnath. When the agreed-upon time expired, Samson whistled a merry tune as he strutted on his way to claim his wife.

He took the shortcut through the vineyards again and stopped to inspect the carcass of the lion he had killed. The carcass had been stripped of flesh, and bees had nested inside the remains. Samson again stretched the limit of his Nazarite vow and ate some honey from the hive (Numbers 6:1-6). He took some of the honey to his parents, who again had taken the arduous route to Timnath for the wedding. He told no one about the lion or the beehive.

According to the custom, Samson gave a festive, seven-day celebration, feasting and making merry with the wedding party and their guests. Thirty Philistine companions joined in the celebration. Samson felt flattered and superior, so he challenged them with a riddle. "If you can solve my riddle by the end of the week, I will give each of you a shirt and a change of clothes. If you cannot solve the riddle, you must give me thirty shirts and changes of clothes," Samson said. "Out of the eater came forth meat, and out of the strong came forth sweetness." He gloated for three days while the companions scratched their heads and bantered for the answer.

At last they grew desperate and decided to resort to tough measures to get the answer. They threatened Samson's bride, "Either you get Samson to tell you the answer, or we will burn your father's house with you and your father in it. Have you called us to your wedding to rob us? Is that not so?"

Samson, the Weak Superman

"Absolutely not," she protested. "Neither my father nor I know anything about that riddle."

"Well, you better find out, or you will be roasted," they sneered.

The girl was terrified and could not quit weeping. Samson was concerned about her happiness and asked, "What is wrong? Aren't you enjoying the feast?"

"Of course I was until it occurred to me that you do not really love me," she sniffled. "Lovers do not keep secrets from each other. This entire time you've boasted about your unsolvable riddle, and you have not told me. If you really loved me, you would tell me the answer." She melted into peevish tears and coy pouting. "I believe that you hate me," she wailed.

"Oh, no! Darling, I do not hate you. I do love you very much. But as for the riddle, I haven't told anyone, not even my parents." The wedding festivities became disastrous. The days dragged on with the same performance from the frightened bride. She refused Samson any pleasure of a smile or any tender moments of love. He was rattled out of sorts. Finally, on the seventh day, the last day of the feast, he told her the answer. She hurriedly told the groomsmen, who swaggered into the great hall, where the feast was about to reach its finale. Samson eagerly waited the closing of the ceremony to claim his new clothes and to sweep his bride to their honeymoon suite.

"Um, er, well, we have one last matter to settle before we leave this wonderful occasion," the best man said. "That's the matter of Samson's riddle. It has been

Nevertheless, God

a tough one, but I believe I have found the answer." With a flourish he bowed to the groom with a condescending smile. He said, "What is sweeter than honey? And what is stronger than a lion?"

Samson blew his top. He exploded in rage. "If you had not plowed with my heifer, you would not have found the answer!" He glared at his bride and spat contempt for her betrayal. He stormed out and said, "I will return with your garments." In his anger, Samson went to Ashkelon, a principal city of the Philistines. The Spirit of the LORD came upon him, and he slew thirty of the male citizens there. He stripped them of their clothes and returned to Timnath. He gave the wedding companions the clothes and, still in a rage, left. He went home to his parents, leaving his wife unfulfilled at Timnath.

"Wow! I believe your groom has abandoned you forever," the best man said. "Too bad, dear," he cajoled, "too bad. But, really, he was not your type, not one of our kind." He oozed to the pretty, young women and took her hand. "Now, I would really make you a wonderful husband. How about it? You wouldn't be happy married to anyone but me anyway." He flirtatiously scooped the woman up and danced her around until she collapsed in laughter. "See, you are happy already," he cheered, "happy to be rid of that bloke, Samson, and thrilled to accept my proposal!"

Her father sensed the opportunity to save face and to save the day. "Since we are all dressed and the feast is over, why not accept the proposal, dear? I suppose that Samson does not love you anyway," her father reasoned.

"He called you a heifer and left without pledging the wedding vows or claiming you as his wife. Your friend, who was your best man for that wedding, has expressed his desire to marry you. Let's just assume that your wedding feast was in celebration of commitment to him."

She agreed, and the ceremony was concluded with the switching of grooms. The couple set up housekeeping in her father's house.

Back in Zorah, Samson's temper and disgust had waned. He began to regret his having left his bride in such an angry huff. Samson looked across his father's wheat fields at the reapers, bending, cutting wheat, and binding sheaves into large shocks to be gathered for winnowing and then stored in barns. His own back ached from the constant bending, cutting, tying, lifting, and stacking sheaves of grain. He was bored and longed for his woman's arms to caress his tired muscles. Abruptly, he left the harvesters and returned to the house, where he showered and got spiffed up to court his woman.

In Timnath, Samson knocked on the familiar door and was surprised by the reception. "I have come for my wife," Samson said.

The father of Samson's woman was startled to see him. "Samson! I thought you had divorced yourself from my daughter. I thought you hated her, so I gave her to your best man and they were married." The man scrambled to recover his advantage. He shifted from one foot to the other. His eyes were riveted on Samson, sizing up the younger man's reaction. He saw Samson was about to explode. "But, Samson, her younger sister is much

Nevertheless, God

prettier than she. You can marry her instead."

Samson seethed inside. He worked his jaws in agitation as thoughts swirled through his head. He ground his teeth in anger and spat out his fury, "I shall be more blameless than the Philistines even though I shall get revenge for this betrayal." He stormed to the woods bordering the nearby grain fields, vineyards, and olive trees. He caught three hundred foxes and pinioned them in pairs. He tied their tails together with a firebrand between the tails. When he had the hundred and fifty pairs of foxes geared for revenge, he set the torches on fire and set the foxes loose. The animals ran through the grain fields, the olive groves, and the vineyards in leaping, thrashing fury to escape the fiery torment while scattering destruction in their wake.

The rising smoke and flames aroused the unsuspecting Philistines' ire. "Arson!" they declared. "Who has burnt our crops?" they demanded.

An informant who had knowledge of Samson's return spoke, "Samson, the son-in-law of the Timnite, did this because his wife was given to another man, who was Samson's companion."

"They shall pay for this!" the angry mob swore. They rushed the house of the guilty man and his daughter. They kicked in the door and dragged the two away. "Tie them to a stake. Burn them like our crops were torched!" they screamed. The firewood was piled around the two, and the torch set it ablaze. They declared, "Now Samson will be satisfied since justice has been done for his having been wronged."

Samson, the Weak Superman

Samson had watched the proceedings from a distance. His anger continued to boil. He was not at all satisfied with that verdict. He said, "Though you have burnt them, yet I will be avenged of you. After that, I will cease venting revenge." He waded among the mob and began slamming bodies together and punching the life out of them in such swift actions no one could escape him. He flung corpses aside like sticks in a great slaughter of Philistines. When his fury was spent, Samson stalked away to live in the top of the rock, Etam, near Bethlehem of Judah.

The Philistines marshaled an army, charged into Judah, and camped in Lehi to plan their attack against Samson. The men of Judah were very worried, "Why have you invaded our land?"

"We have come to capture Samson, for he has not only burnt our crops but also has killed many of our men. We intend to do to him as he has done to us."

"Hold your forces," the men of Judah replied. "We will deliver Samson to you if you will take him and leave peacefully."

"That we will do," the Philistine commander answered. "Our quarrel is only with that one man and not with you."

Three thousand men of Judah marched up the hill to the top of the rock, Etam. They found Samson's nook and informed him, "Don't you know that the Philistines rule over us? They have invaded our land, seeking revenge. See what you have done to us by coming here?"

"I have done to them exactly what they did to

me," Samson said.

"We have come to arrest you and to take you bound to the Philistines. Then they will retreat and leave us alone."

"I will go with you only if you swear that you will not kill me yourselves."

"No, we won't kill you, but we will bind you and take you to the Philistines," they promised. Samson surrendered to the men of Judah and allowed them to tie him with two new ropes. They took him from the rock to the waiting Philistines at Lehi.

Samson willingly followed the charade of handing him prisoner to the Philistines. He stood bound and appeared subdued before the enemy. The Philistines began a victory rally. They praised their god for capturing Samson. A great shout of mocking, repulsive threats were hurled at him. The Spirit of the LORD came mightily upon Samson. He broke the cords as if they had been charred flax. With both hands loose, he could defend himself against the charging throng of Philistines. Looking for something to use as a club, Samson saw a discarded, moist jawbone of a donkey nearby. He picked it up and began to flay it right and left, mowing the Philistines down as they surged forward. Corpses piled in heaps around Samson. With no one left to slay, Samson threw the jawbone aside and sat to rest. "From now on, this place shall be called the place of the cast-away jawbone," he said as he viewed the heaps of dead Philistines.

He licked his parched lips and heaved tired shoulders. "I'm so thirsty I could die," he moaned. Then he

Samson, the Weak Superman

prayed, "LORD, You have given this great deliverance to me, but now am I to die of thirst and fall into Philistine hands?" Samson looked at the jawbone he had thrown on the ground. Something strange was happening to that bone. Suddenly, a carving action hollowed a cup into the bone, making it into a dipper. Immediately it was full of water! Samson drank his fill and thanked God. He then remarked, "I shall now call this 'the well of him that cried.' " En–hakkore in Lehi remained the name to mark that occurrence of a miracle. Israel accepted Samson as their deliverer and did not try to arrest him again.

Samson still did not seem to curb his wandering lust for heathen women. The event with the woman at Timnath did not teach him a thing. Samson arrogantly went down to Gaza, the largest cluster of the Philistine people. He saw a harlot advertising her trade, and his passion flamed out of control. He went home with her to spend the night reveling in sin. The Philistines recognized Samson and posted a stakeout at the city gate. Armed men surrounded the city and quietly waited for dawn. "We will kill him when he tries to leave in the morning," they said.

Samson had his fill of the harlot, and at midnight he decided to leave. He walked unchallenged until he reached the doors in the city's gate. Finding the doors locked and the sleeping guards around, Samson knew he had to flee. Without so much as a grunt, Samson braced himself under the door frame and heaved the doors and the two posts, along with the long bar that secured the doors shut, upon his shoulders and walked out of the

Nevertheless, God

city. The sound of ripping wood and the grinding of a heavy object being carried over the graveled entrance woke the guards. They were so stunned at the sight that they could only watch Samson as he walked away with their city gate doors. Samson knew soldiers waited to kill him outside those gates. Using the large gates as a shield, Samson calmly walked through the hole in the wall, and the strong man kept walking for miles down the road. He climbed to the top of a hill near the Israelite city of Hebron. There he deposited that load.

From Hebron Samson traveled to the valley of Sorek. The valley produced very desirable vineyards in the tribe of Judah. However, the Philistines had retaken the valley and occupied it. Samson again fell in love with a Philistine woman, Delilah. Her name denotes that she was a delicate woman, but she was very seductive and deceptively greedy for money. When her countrymen learned that she had taken up with Samson, they concocted a plan to entrap Samson and to destroy him. With the huge Philistine treasury financing the plan, Delilah was easily persuaded to cooperate.

"You must persuade Samson to trust you with his secret formula for such super strength. That shouldn't be hard for such a beautiful and clever woman as you," they flattered. Delilah reveled in the pomp and diplomacy of her mission. She determined to have full pleasure in obtaining that reward. The head of the Philistine house of lords continued, "We of the house of lords will each give you eleven hundred pieces of silver if you can discover wherein his strength lies and by what means we may prevail against him. We want to bind him and to afflict him. This man must be taken out." Delilah smiled coyly and agreed. The contract was guaranteed in writing, and the dignitaries left her to work her wiles.

Dreams of all that money and how she could use it activated her feminine wiles. She seductively played Samson with charm and sweetness. "Samson, tell me what makes you so strong. Just look at those muscles! You are the envy of every man who sees you. I am so lucky to enjoy your love and the pleasure of your company. How on earth could a little ol' woman like me possibly match you for desirability? Tell me, what is your secret? Maybe I could profit from the formula. We could make a fetching pair if I knew your secret to buffing up my figure to match your handsome body."

Daily, Delilah turned on the charm. When charm alone did not work, she turned on the cajoling tears. She fluttered her teary eyelids and stroked his long tresses. It became an obsession that consumed her. Every moment together with Samson was spent on the ploy to break his spirit. At first, Samson played along with Delilah, treating the issue as a game. He began toying with Delilah. "If you bind me with seven cords that have not dried, I shall be weak like another man," he told her. There was just a hint of truth in the story; seven cords for seven locks of hair chalked one hint into the answer she sought.

Delilah placed an order for the new, moist cords and notified the Philistine lords. They brought the money and hid in the closets of her house when Samson arrived home. That night she playfully bound Samson as he lay asleep. The cords were as tight as she possibly could tie them. She shook Samson in a panic. "The Philistines are here to take you!" she cried. The lords burst confidently from hiding. Samson was startled to see that his bedroom was full of men ready to kill him. He jumped out of bed, breaking the new cords as if they were tow touched with fire. He laughed at the Philistines, who stumbled over each other in a mad rush for the door. He mocked them as they fled.

Delilah then played the role of an offended, nagging wife, "You mocked me and told me lies. I implore you to quit lying and to tell me how you may be bound."

Samson thought of another lie to tease Delilah and to make a mockery of the lords. "If they bind me fast with new ropes that have never been used, I shall be weak like another man."

Again, after Samson was asleep, Delilah followed his instructions with new ropes, fresh from the rope maker. She poked him in the ribs and said, "Samson, the Philistines are here to take you." The eager lords were ready to pounce when Samson flexed his muscles and broke those ropes like thread. They fled in terror again with a glaring glance at Delilah. Samson had given another tiny clue, the new ropes which had never been cut or customized for any particular use.

The pesky woman feigned hurt and embarrassment. She wept and fell upon Samson in passionate pleading, "You have mocked me again. You told me lies. If you love me, you must be honest with me. Wherein does your strength lie? How might you be bound?"

Samson, the Weak Superman

Another day of nagging and tears of feigned hurt ended when Samson boldly told her another story. "If you weave the seven locks of my hair with the web, I will become weak," Samson declared before yawning.

Delilah stroked his long locks and sweetly rubbed his back until he was sleeping soundly. Having surety that Samson was very tired and most likely dead to the world, she took her threaded loom to the bed. She began the task of weaving his hair like woolen threads into the tapestry she had already strung on the loom. The shuttle went back and forth, back and forth until the hair was securely woven as fabric. The apparatus hung from Samson's head like some grotesque hat. Delilah smiled over the deftness of her weaving skills. Her lover had not stirred during the whole ordeal. "Samson, the Philistines are upon you!" she cried in alarm. Samson scrambled to his feet and went away, with the weaving pin and the web bouncing on his shoulders.

The ignorance and calloused indifference portrayed in the relationship between Samson and Delilah depicts absolute, blind lust in both Samson and Delilah. He desired flesh; she desired money. Samson had not developed a committed relationship with God. His was based entirely upon his parents' encounter with an angel. He had not sought God for his own experience. His physical strength had certainly been tested, but the mettle of his inner character and will had not. The lust of flesh overpowered Samson's weak commitment to honor and to obey God. His resolve wore thin, and he caved after days of constant badgering and baiting his lust. Delilah made continuing attempts to learn his secret. "How can you say you love me when your heart is not with me? You're not honest with me. You have mocked me three times and have yet to tell wherein is your great strength."

Samson longed for peace. He longed for simple affection from his companion without all the harangue. So he told her the secret, "There has never been a razor on my head. I have been a Nazarite to God since birth. If I am shaven, my strength will be gone from me. I will become weak as other men."

The truth rang solidly with Delilah. She sent word to the lords of the Philistines, "Bring your money. This time Samson has come clean with me. I know his secret. He will be ready for you to bind him tonight." The house of lords adjourned early, and they withdrew the money from the vault. With the cash jingling in bank bags, they arrived at Delilah's door at the appointed time.

In the meantime, Samson had a filling dinner and looked forward to a good night of pleasure and sleep. The nagging had ceased, and Delilah was happy. She smiled and was so romantic that she curled up on the couch and suggested that he relax while she kissed and caressed him, massaged his scalp, and promised him sweet love. Samson did relax with his head cradled in her lap of death. He never knew when the fingers quit massaging and the barber started clipping his hair at the scalp. It all was done so gently. The bald head reflected the glare of candlelight in the room. The long tresses lay like a discarded halo on the floor. Delilah began to tease him with pinches and punches of her own to test his strength. When her curiosity was satisfied that Samson actually suffered pain from her tormenting assault, she called for the lords. "The Philistines are here to take you, Samson!" she mocked with glee. The lords converged like vultures upon Samson. He strode from the room and shook himself as he had before, not knowing that the LORD had departed from him.

The Philistine lords attacked him and quickly overpowered him. They tied him and hauled him to their prison. There they tortured him and burned his eyes out with hot pokers. They tied him to the grinding wheel at their mill. He was forced to push that wheel around like an ox. Day after day he suffered their taunts and mockery. Day after day he was tortured and made to grind their grain. Days followed nights, and Samson prayed prayers of regret and repentance as he suffered alone in his prison of stone and darkness. Slowly his hair began to grow. He could feel the stubble when he wiped sweat from his head. As his hair grew, so did his confidence in God. He had become a trophy of triumph for the house of lords in the Philistine capital of Gaza. Though he wore shackles of brass, his spirit roamed free to communicate with the LORD God of Israel. His hair grew so that it fell over his forehead, dripping sweat down his face. The Philistines did not notice any change in Samson. When his seven locks of hair had fully grown, Samson realized that hope was not lost forever.

On a special holiday for the Philistines, the entire country came to Gaza to celebrate in the large arena dedicated to Dagon, their god. Sacrifices were offered to

Nevertheless, God

Dagon, and their prized sport featured Samson the strong man. The master of ceremonies announced, "And now, we show you Samson the strong man of Israel, who was the destroyer of our country and the slayer of many of our citizens. Here he is, folks! Look at him now!" He was paraded in his ragged state to the center of the arena, led by a young boy. The jeers, the laughter, the praises to Dagon for Samson's captivity filled the arena with thunderous applause. Samson was forced to make sport for the crazed crowd. He finally was allowed to sit between the two pillars which held up the roof.

Samson spoke softly to the child. "Lead me to the two support pillars so I can demonstrate my strength," he meekly asked. Unsuspectingly, the child led him to the pillars. The thousands of Philistines joked and jeered as Samson leaned first upon one post and then upon the other, memorizing the size and distance between the two. Samson bowed his head in what the enemy judged as humiliation, but God saw it as humility and prayer. "O Lord GOD, remember me, I pray. Strengthen me, I pray, only once more. O God, let me at once be avenged of the Philistines for my two eyes." He placed his hands on each of the posts, began to pull with all his might, and yelled, "God, let me die with the Philistines!" The arena began collapsing in a sudden, thunderous crash of devastation. The Philistines were crushed to death inside the arena, and three thousand plunged to their death from the roof. Samson also was crushed by the fall of the temple to Dagon. The melee of falling bodies and massive timbers made escape impossible. Thus, Samson killed more

Samson, the Weak Superman

Philistines in his death than he did in his lifetime.

The men of Samson's hometown heard of his death. They went to Gaza to dig through the rubble to find his body. They took the mangled form of Israel's judge and buried him in the family cemetery. The summary of Samson's judgeship was in the absence of what he could have done to deliver Israel if he would have learned self-control and obedience to God and to his calling. He accredited his super strength to his prowess and believed his Nazarite vow was the means of his strength rather than any commitment and relationship with God. Therefore, he lost both the gift and the Giver.

Samson was the right man for the job. He had the absolute calling of God and the anointing of God. He had the supernatural strength from God to do exploits. He had the right family genealogy. He was taught the right, godly values from infancy. He had everything he needed to be the greatest and the most powerful deliverer Israel ever had since Joshua. He proved that singlehandedly he could match the enemy and prevail. But he failed! His demise began as seeds of lust, which were sown as wild oats, became a deliberate lifestyle of pleasure. His lack of self-control cost Israel a terrible shortfall in deliverance from Philistine domination. He left that thorn to grow and to reproduce misery for Israel throughout history. What an epitaph for one who should have and could have been the greatest!

Chapter 11

Jonathan, a Displaced Levite Judge

After the death of Samson, the story of Israel's judges continued with a curious incident that happened to the tribes Ephraim and Dan because of a Levite. The young Levite left his home in Bethlehem of the tribe of Judah and went looking for employment and a place to live. He inadvertently got enmeshed in a family's religious feud.

A man of Ephraim named Micah was a thief. He filched eleven hundred silver coins from his mother's purse. She cursed and fumed about the robbery to her son. Micah's conscience was scorched by his mother's rage against the thief. Guilt forced him to confess the theft, "Mother, the money that was taken from you, I have it. I took it." Micah handed her the loot.

His mother was shocked but so relieved that the money was returned that she pronounced a blessing upon him, "Blessed are you of the LORD, my son. I had wholly dedicated that silver unto the LORD from me for you. I want a graven image and a molten image made with the money. So take the money, and make the images. They will be yours." The woman thrust the coins back into her son's pockets. Now, all of Israel had been taught the

Nevertheless, God

LORD'S commandment that Israel should not make any graven images.

Micah protested, "No, Mother, you should take the money, and do whatever you want with it. Have it shaped into whatever you wish." The woman took the money and gave it to a founder.

"Here are two hundred shekels of silver," she said and poured the coins from her purse. "Now, make a graven image and a molten image from these." She kept nine hundred silver coins from that which she had declared to be wholly dedicated to the LORD, for reasons not ever stated. However, the cheap images were made contrary to the holy commandments of the LORD, and evidently nothing was ever given into the treasury of the Tabernacle of the LORD. The woman made a house of gods for her son and put the images on display. In the shrine was also an ephod and a teraphim. Micah dedicated one of his sons to be the priest. The young priest buckled the ephod around his waist and kept the teraphim dusted so as to catch the attention of those who entered the house of gods.

A disclaimer was written to this story in Judges 17:6: "In those days there was no king in Israel, but every man did that which was right in his own eyes." Situational ethics had produced a generation who had left the old paths of seeking God's way. The commandments given by God to govern Israel were housed far away in the Tabernacle and forgotten by the common household in Israel.

Into that mess entered the Levite in his move from

Bethlehem to wherever. He knocked on Micah's door, seeking lodging. Micah welcomed him into his home. The application for lodging disclosed that the guest was a Levite. "How wonderful!" exclaimed Micah upon hearing the news. "I have need of a real, ordained priest to become pastor of our local church. Are you looking for a job?"

A big smile brightened the Levite's face. "As a matter of fact, I am," he announced.

"Then you have the position. Your responsibilities will relieve my novice of a son from his temporary appointment. I'll show you our church. I will pay you ten shekels of silver per year if you will become my personal spiritual counselor and priest. You will have room and board provided and a new suit every year," Micah promised. He then introduced the Levite to the constituents and showed him the shrine.

"I am delighted to take the position," the Levite accepted with no haggling. His duties began immediately. He loved his new position and fulfilled his job satisfactorily. Micah was most pleased with his new priest. Micah was so delighted to have the Levite that he treated him as a son. Micah consecrated the Levite, meaning that he was made full-time pastor without the need to hold a secular job.

"Now I know that the LORD will do me good, seeing that I have a Levite as my priest," Micah boasted.

In the meantime, the people of the tribe of Dan felt cramped in a land shortage. They went searching for more real estate to acquire. They had not carved out their inheritance from the Canaanites as instructed by Moses and Joshua. In the search for property, the five men from Eshtaol and Zorah, Samson's home, stopped at Micah's house in Mount Ephraim. They heard conversation before they knocked on the door. One said, "I recognize that voice. He is a Levite from Bethlehem. We can ask advice of the LORD to prosper us in our mission."

The men were welcomed, and they joined in worship at Micah's shrine. The men were impressed and asked, "Who brought you here? What salary do you make? What do you have here in your shrine? We want you to ask counsel of the LORD for us. We promise to reward you for your services."

The Levite replied, "Micah has been good to me, like a father. He hired me to be his priest, and I am happy to be of service to you." He did inquire of the LORD for the men and said, "Go in peace. Before the LORD is the way you are in."

The five spies left and traveled to Laish. The place was quiet, peaceful, and secluded far from the Zidonians. No magistrate ruled in the land to shame them for their careless living, and no business transpired between Laish and her neighbors. The spies marked the area for their next acquisition. Then, they returned home to employ enough men to turn Laish into a residence for the tribe of Dan. With persuasion, they reported, "We have seen the land. It is good, and we can easily take it. Waste no time in closing the deal. It is a large place and the people are secure, but God has given the land to us. And, by the way, there is no shortage of anything the earth can pro-

Jonathan, a Displaced Levite Judge

vide in the place." Right away, six hundred men packed their gear and marched toward Laish. En route they approached Micah's house. The five spies said, "In this man's place are an ephod, a teraphim, a graven image, a molten image, and a Levite priest. Now, consider what you have to do."

The priest looked out his window and saw the warriors approaching. He recognized the five spies. They exchanged greetings of peace. The six hundred warriors posted themselves at the entrance of the gate with their weapons ready. The spies entered Micah's house of gods, stole the sacred icons, and kidnaped the priest. Before Micah knew what had happened, they were leaving with his sacred loot. The priest had protested the looting and his kidnaping, but threats silenced him. "Hold your peace and your tongue," they warned. "You are to be a counselor and a priest for the tribe of Dan now. Isn't that better than being a priest to one man's house?" The young man relaxed and thought about his good fortune and promotion.

The company was well on the way out of sight when Micah caught up with them. The dust kicked up behind the drove of men and cattle as Micah and his hurriedly mustered posse of Ephraimites blocked the road and shouted, "Stop!"

"What ails you, Micah, that you come with such a company?" the soldiers remarked.

"You stole my gods, which I made, and my priest has been kidnaped. I have nothing left, and you ask what ails me?" Micah pleaded.

Nevertheless, God

The men of Dan growled, "Don't utter another word. If you complain again, some of us just may get angry and kill you and your family."

Micah backed away in fear. He had sized up the situation and knew he could not force the issue. The six hundred soldiers with their captives and loot marched to Laish, herding their captives, the children in the carriage, and the cattle before them. They attacked and burned the city of Laish. All the residents were slaughtered. The Danites cleared the debris, rebuilt the city, and named it Dan. A special shrine was built for Micah's images. The priest was appointed to serve in the new shrine. Jonathan the son of Gershom (a Levite), the son of Manasseh, and his sons were priests to the tribe of Dan for many years, all the time the Tabernacle of the LORD was in Shiloh (Judges 18:18-31).

The tribe of Levi had no territorial boundaries. That tribe had been scattered through all the twelve tribes of Israel and lived in designated cities and suburbs.

Chapter 12
An Anonymous Levite Judge

Like the previous one, the following story seems out of context with the other judges. Chapters 17, 18, 19, 20, and 21 of Judges veer from the recording of particular deliverers who arose to deliver Israel from external enemies. However, the Book of Judges also reveals Israel's internal problems and conflicts. Domestic trouble was attributed to the lack of a central leader and base of government. As rudderless as Israel seemed to have become, God did not leave her without the testimony of His Word. The holy Tabernacle, erected in Shiloh under Joshua's leadership, had remained there all during those tumultuous years. The anointed priest of God had remained on duty and had kept the law of God. But Israel had drifted from acknowledging theocratic authority from the Tabernacle as absolute. The Levites had been scattered throughout the nation of Israel, and only the descendants of Aaron had maintained households close to the Tabernacle.

Judges 20:27-28 denotes the time period in which this story occurred. It was when Phinehas, the grandson of Aaron, was priest in Shiloh. Phinehas had performed a purging feat in a sex scandal at Peor not long before Moses died. Moses pronounced an eternal blessing upon Phinehas for his swift action to rid Israel from her evil

Nevertheless, God

(Numbers 25:1-13).

However, Eleazar, Phinehas' father, was high priest at the time of Peor. Phinehas became high priest about the close of Joshua's leadership and after the death of Eleazar about thirty years after Israel entered Canaan (Joshua 24:33). Since the accounts of the judges covered hundreds of years, this story was not filed in Scripture in its proper sequential order of events. Judges 11:26-27 informs that Jephthah's judgeship occurred three hundred years after Israel had possessed the land she conquered east of the Jordan River in a conquest which had been accomplished about two years before Moses died. Afterward, Joshua led Israel for approximately thirty years in Canaan across the river. With that understanding, it is determined that this story took place after Joshua was dead and when the elders serving under him were in charge. It was in those later years Israel began to rely on judges to give them direction (Deuteronomy 16:18; 17:9). Because Phinehas was a recognized, capable leader under Joshua's ministry, a particular judge was not in charge of Israel at the time of this story. The priest, Phinehas, was the accepted leader.

An unnamed Levite took for himself a common-law wife from Bethlehem, Judah. She was unhappy with her marriage and had an affair. Then, she returned to her father. Four months later the Levite husband discovered where she was and went to get her back. The man and his servant saw the woman before they reached the house. The Levite spoke friendly to her, hoping to patch their relationship and to convince her to return with him to

An Anonymous Levite Judge

Mount Ephraim. She was persuaded and led the two men to her father, who was overjoyed to see his son-in-law. "You must stay with me while you are in town," he said.

The Levite was pressed to stay longer than he had intended because his father-in-law hosted a wine party each evening. The Levite was too hung over to travel those days. But on the fifth day, the Levite got out of bed early and declared that he was leaving. The host again protested, "There is no need for you to leave so soon. Come. Have more wine with me."

The Levite drank until time was lost for hours. Through the fog of a wine-induced haze, the Levite realized the sun had slipped toward its resting place. He was startled and declared, "I must be leaving. I should have left hours ago. Hurry up, wife dear. We must be going." The three people left Bethlehem under the protesting father's urging to stay one more night. They traveled until evening shades colored the western horizon.

The servant said, "Master, come, I pray, and let us take lodging in Jebus for the night. We are close enough to get inside the city before dark." Jebus was the city which the tribe of Judah had burned and left abandoned and which the heathen had repossessed and rebuilt as a fortified stronghold.

"No. We will not lodge in a city of the Jebusite strangers. We will try to make it to Gibeah, one of the cities of Israel. If we can't lodge in Gibeah, we can stay in Ramah." The Levite's party pushed on, racing the sun. Near Gibeah of the tribe of Benjamin, the sun dipped behind the hilltops, and night swallowed the road. "We will stay in Gibeah tonight," the Levite said. They exited the road and entered Gibeah as the last straggling farmers returned from their fields. The Levite inquired about lodging, but nothing was available. The little party prepared to bed down in the street.

As the city's gate was closing, a farmer trudged through and the gate clanged shut. The street was otherwise deserted, for the citizens had begun to eat supper and to prepare for bed. The weary farmer saw the pitiful trio stranded in the street. "What is your problem? You are strangers here, I see. Where are you going, and where did you come from?" he asked.

"I went from Mount Ephraim to Bethlehem, Judah, and now I am just passing through, going to the house of the LORD. No one has given me lodging, so we are stuck in the street. However, I do have enough food for the donkeys and enough bread and wine for us. All we need is a place to rest and a stable for my donkeys for the night."

The farmer smiled, "I am from Mount Ephraim as well. I came to live for a while among the folk of Benjamin. I have a little farm plot in the countryside. It provides well enough for an old man such as I. Come on home with me. I have plenty to share with you and your animals. Please don't spend the night in the street. It is not safe." He cautiously nodded toward the curious men eavesdropping nearby. The old man led the party to his modest home, and they fed the donkeys and bedded them. Then they proceeded into the house for supper. As they were enjoying the meal and merry conversation,

An Anonymous Levite Judge

there was a banging on the door. The old man peeked out the door. "A mob rings my house!" he said. "What do you want?" he called from behind the bolted door.

The men of the city demanded, "We want that man you brought home. He'll be fresh pleasure for our orgies tonight."

The old gentleman slipped outside to reason with the perverts. "No, no, my fellow citizens. Do not do such wickedness. That man is a guest of mine. Don't do such folly. My unmarried daughter and my guest's common-law wife are here. I'll bring them out for you. Do whatever you desire with them, but do not harm this man."

"Do as we ask, old man," they demanded.

The Levite heard the old man's pleadings. When the man's daughter paled and shook in fear for her health, her future, and her life, the Levite took charge. He took his wife's hand and pulled her through the door as he addressed the mob, "Here is my wife." He gritted his teeth and pushed her forward. The men fell on her like hungry dogs pouncing upon a piece of meat. The perverts dragged her to their occult worship center. Their frenzied orgies began. All night they abused and molested her repeatedly. When the dawn streaked the eastern sky, they set her free. The suffering woman found her way back to the house where her husband lodged. After staggering through the streets of Gibeah, she collapsed at the door of the house with her hand reaching for the door. The Levite arose at dawn to be on his way. He opened the door, and there lay his wife on the threshold. "Get up. It is time to be gone," he said. "Wake up."

Nevertheless, God

The woman did not respond. The Levite picked up her lifeless body and laid her across his donkey's back. Heartsick and angry, he traveled to Mount Ephraim. He took the corpse into his house and laid her on a table. With a saw, he butchered her body into twelve pieces. He sent a piece of the body by special express to every tribe of Israel. The message attached was: "The men of Gibeah of the tribe of Benjamin practice perversion and occult worship. They abused and molested my wife until she died. Consider what must be done, and advise me." (Remember the sensual, idolatrous worship to the gods of Nimrod.)

The elders smelled the rotting flesh and gagged, but the message infuriated them. "Nothing like this has been done or seen in Israel since our leaving Egypt until today. What shall be done? Speak your mind. We must do something to avenge that poor man and to punish those of Gibeah." They called a general assembly at Mizpeh, and there before the LORD, at the sacred rock of covenant, they asked God how they should handle the problem. Four hundred thousand armed footmen were gathered around that altar.

The men of Benjamin heard of the assembly at Mizpeh when the Levite was called to testify for himself. "Tell us how this wickedness came about," the chief Israelite men said. The entire gruesome story was told.

The Levite recounted the story, "The men of Gibeah stormed the house that night and would have molested me but were persuaded to take my wife instead. They abused and molested her until she died. You are all

An Anonymous Levite Judge

men of Israel. Tell me what I should do."

Outrage against Gibeah called for a resolution for punishment. "None of us will go home until we have finalized this resolution," the chairman said. "Ten men of every hundred from each tribe of Israel that is assembled here will be drafted for duty. Then a hundred from every thousand and a thousand out of ten thousand will form the supply line for food for the expedition. Our soldiers are to render to Gibeah a punishment equal to her crime. What Gibeah has done to the Levite and his wife is folly against all Israel."

The tribe of Benjamin was warned that the troops were advancing to Gibeah. "The wickedness of the men of Gibeah demands the death sentence. Therefore, deliver those evil men to us that we may put away this evil from Israel." The post served only to unify Benjamin to fight the amassed troops of Israel. This tribe had long before produced the left-handed judge named Ehud. At the time related in this story, Benjamin had become a producer of evil. The men of Benjamin rose as a whole to defend the wicked men of the tribe.

Twenty-six thousand armed men of Benjamin raced to swell Gibeah's defense from a meager seven hundred men. Among those soldiers were seven hundred left-handed men who could sling stones and not miss even the small targets. Israel considered the opposition and the emotional and physical damage a battle would inflict. Therefore, she chose to go to the house of God in Shiloh first and to ask counsel of the LORD. "Which of us shall go up first to fight Benjamin?" they prayed.

Nevertheless, God

The LORD answered, "Judah shall go up first."

Early the next morning, Israel encamped against Gibeah and challenged the city. The militia inside the city swarmed out like angry hornets and slew twenty-two thousand of Israel's troops. Israel licked her wounds and retreated to Shiloh. Again the elders sought counsel from God, "Shall Israel go again to do battle with Benjamin our brother?"

The LORD replied again, "Go up against him." The tribes' army advanced against the city as they had done the previous day. This time, Benjamin's army mowed down eighteen thousand soldiers. That totaled forty thousand men lost from Israel's troops in two days. The morale was very low, and bitterness niggled at the men's confidence. It seemed that the LORD had purposely directed them to a death trap.

The battered troops assembled at the Tabernacle of the LORD again. Phinehas, the priest, led in the intercession. A mourning army fasted and prayed all day. At evening, they offered burnt offerings and peace offerings before the LORD. They meekly asked the LORD before the ark of the covenant of God, "Shall Israel again go up to battle Benjamin my brother, or shall I cease fighting?"

The LORD spoke plainly, "Go up, for tomorrow I will deliver them into your hand."

The top brass drew different plans for their next attack. Some of the troops were sent behind the city to lie in wait until signaled to attack. The others charged the city as they had done previously. The troops of Benjamin came roaring out of the city, wild with confidence that the battle would end as before. Israel retreated, and Benjamin chased them until they were away from the city's wall of protection, killing several soldiers who were retreating to Shiloh and several in the field around Gibeah. The Benjamite army was drawn into the highways in the feigned retreat. The troops behind the city charged from the meadows through the city gates, trapping the army of Benjamin. Ten thousand chosen men of war set Gibeah a blazing inferno. When the pretending retreating Israelite soldiers saw the flames, they turned upon their enemy with such force that Benjamin fled. They ran but could not escape the sword of Israel. Israel enclosed the army of Benjamin and slaughtered eighteen thousand men of valor. In a longer chase toward the wilderness to the east, Benjamin lost another five thousand men. There were two thousand killed in Gibeah. Twenty-five thousand men of Benjamin died in that day's battle.

Six hundred men of Benjamin fled to the wilderness and took refuge in the fortress-like rock of Rimmon for four months. The troops of Israel wrecked the countryside, burning the cities of Benjamin. All the inhabitants were killed and the animals slaughtered as well. The six hundred men of Benjamin were imprisoned in their fortress while Israel destroyed their cities and farms.

When the fury of Israel was spent, she assembled at the choice military camp at Mizpeh before the rock of witness. "None of us will give our daughters to be wives for Benjamin," they declared. They then marched back to Shiloh to the Tabernacle, where they wept and prayed until evening. "O LORD God of Israel, why has it come

Nevertheless, God

to this? Why should one tribe be lacking in Israel?" They repented for their own wrath and for the nearly extinct tribe of Benjamin.

The next day, they built an altar and offered burnt offerings and peace offerings. "Who among all the tribes of Israel did not come with us to the congregation of the LORD? Whoever did not come to Mizpeh shall surely die," the elders said. While Israel continued to repent for Benjamin, the chief men asked, "How shall we provide wives for the men of Benjamin who are in Rimmon? We swore by the LORD that we would not give them our daughters. What shall we do? None of the wives of the men of Benjamin was saved alive in the war."

"Let us tabulate the cities represented here to see which city has not sent delegates. The women from the cities not represented could be taken as wives for the men of Benjamin." The idea was voted upon, and the tabulation divulged that the city of Jabesh–gilead of the tribe of Manasseh was the only city not represented. The assembly sent twelve thousand of their best warriors to Jabesh–gilead with the orders, "Go, smite the citizens of that city, and kill every male and every married woman. Keep only the young virgin girls alive. Bring them back to Shiloh, where we can present them before the LORD to become wives for the men of Benjamin." When the girls arrived, the soldiers were instructed, "Go to the rock Rimmon, and speak peaceably to the men of Benjamin. They can come to Shiloh and take them wives." The transaction was made, but two hundred men were yet without wives. "There must be an inheritance for the

An Anonymous Levite Judge

men of Benjamin who escaped so that a tribe will not be destroyed out of Israel. What other ideas exist?"

"Remember, a feast for single women has been hosted at Shiloh every year. The women are meeting this year in a place north of Bethel on the east side of the highway going up from Bethel to Shechem right south of Lebonah. The men of Benjamin could go there and catch wives for themselves," someone expostulated.

"An excellent proposition!" the entire assembly agreed. The two hundred men of Benjamin were sent to the Single Women's Retreat to hide themselves near the camp until the women were all enjoying the festivities. "Hide in the vineyards, and when the daughters of Shiloh come to dance, catch yourself a wife and take her back to Benjamin. When the girls' fathers complain, we will say, 'Be favorable to the men of Benjamin for our sakes because we didn't save any of their women alive in the war. If you won't give them wives at this time, you shall be held guilty.'" The men did as instructed and captured brides. They returned to their burned cities, rebuilt them, and repopulated the tribe of Benjamin. The other tribal warriors returned to their homes, and Israel continued to do what was right in every man's eyes because there was no king nor central leader to give direction.

A note to clarify: Before there was a king in Israel, Samuel had lived in Shiloh at the Tabernacle with Eli the high priest. He had access to all the records of Israel for hundreds of years from Moses forward. The writings of both Moses and Joshua had been preserved in the Tabernacle along with the records of various scribes afterward.

Nevertheless, God

However, the events of the Levites had always been chronicled and guarded more cautiously than most records because of the belief Israel held that the bloodline of Levi would always be sacred and that the direct descendants of Aaron were the only rightful priests to hold the position of high priest. They alone had the most sacred right to enter the Holiest of Holies inside the veil of the Tabernacle where the ark of the LORD was kept. From the ark the presence of the LORD emitted a visible semblance of His presence among Israel. The Levites and the priests had been given the task of guardians of the law of God and keepers of His Tabernacle. Thus, the last two, seemingly unorthodox, stories of Judges were preserved for history not because the Levites involved had been deliverers from outside enemies of Israel but because they had been chosen by God to protect, to preserve, and to implement the law of God. Therefore, most Bible scholars ascribe the compilation of the Book of Judges to Samuel.

CHAPTER 13

RUTH, AN UNLIKELY MOTHER OF THE ETERNAL JUDGE

Ruth was a heathen woman, God's Nevertheless to birth the bloodline for the eternal Judge. Her story took place during the time of the judges of Israel and probably was recorded by her great-grandson, King David. Ruth 1:1 states, "Now it came to pass in the days when the judges ruled, that there was a famine in the land." That background, along with the birth records of the families of Israel, gives a clue of the time frame for the events (Ruth 4:16-22; Matthew 1:4-6). Israel was in Canaan when Salmon married Rahab, the harlot of Jericho who had hidden the spies of Israel. That marriage produced Boaz, who married Ruth. Therefore, the story of Ruth must have taken place within a hundred to a hundred and fifty years after Israel settled Canaan. According to Jephthah, his judgeship began three hundred years after Israel had conquered Sihon and Og before crossing Jordan River into Canaan (Judges 11:26).

Since Jephthah was not the last judge recorded in the Book of Judges and there are only two generations separating Ruth from David, it may be reasonably determined that Ruth lived during the time of peace with Moab after Ehud brought rest to Israel for eighty years

Nevertheless, God

(Judges 3:29-30). Several of the judges mentioned in Scripture were contemporary, ruling in different tribes or even across Jordan River from each other.

The beautiful story of Ruth is not validated by the exact date of its occurrence but rather by God's promise. The story interjects into the genealogical account of Israel's progression in Canaan a surprising resurrection of the promise of Genesis 3:15 when God said, "I will put enmity between thee [the serpent] and the woman, and between thy seed and her seed; it shall bruise thy head, and thou shalt bruise his heel." During a bleak period of Israel's existence, God sprinkled a reminder that the promise was still alive. Not only was the promise alive, but it was secreted in Moab, a heathenish descendant of Lot, Abraham's nephew. No judge or prophet of Israel had expected that promise in such an abominable place in a non-Abrahamic descendant. However, God had kept track of that seed of promise, and He brought it into play at the right time. Like the discovery of a local hero, Ruth oozed into the stream of prophecy. She sought no limelight, no acclaim of heroism, not even a place of her own. Pure love and commitment to her mother-in-law, Naomi, swept her into that eternal stream. She desired only to serve that woman who led her from idolatry into the knowledge of JEHOVAH, the God of Israel.

The seed of the woman was put in place in Bethlehem as a spiritual covert operation. The common Israelite of that day was totally unaware of God's intervention for the seed of promise. The spiritual leaders and judges were not aware of it. There were no genealogical birth

Ruth, an Unlikely Mother . . .

records for that promised seed so that its lineage could be pinpointed. In the annals of time, Israel had polluted her faith to follow God beyond Moses and Joshua. The sad chroniclers of history wrote of cycles of revival, then sin and oppression. Ruth was introduced into the history of Bethlehem, the tiny village of country folk, shepherds, farmers, and a few merchants, an unlikely place to give rise to the eternal Judge.

Fields of grain framed the hamlet. The shepherds tended flocks of sheep on the hills surrounding the town. Bethlehem was of no recognizable consequence to Israel as a whole. When famine came, Elimelech felt no obligation to stay in the village. He fled starvation and sought greener pastures and better opportunities for his sons, Mahlon and Chilion. He and Naomi moved the family across the Jordan River to the heathen land of Moab, where the god Chemosh was revered as supreme. They found some contentment and acceptance in Moab. The boys grew to manhood and found lovely brides of Moab. Naomi enjoyed the daughters-in-law. She was satisfied and fulfilled until tragedy left the three women widows ten years after the family left Bethlehem. Elimelech had been a man of means, but his death and the death of the sons left their wives in poverty (Ruth 1:20-21).

Naomi received word from home that the famine had passed in Israel. She decided to return to Bethlehem. The three women traveled a short way together when Naomi began to complain, "You girls go home to your mothers. You have been kind to me, so may the LORD grant you rest and other husbands in your parents' homes." She kissed them both, and they all wept.

Orpah and Ruth said through tears, "We will go with you to your people."

Naomi protested again, "Go home to your parents. Why would you want to go with me? I have no hope of having any more sons for you to marry. Even if I did, would you wait for them to grow up so you could marry them? No, it would be best for you to return to your people. It grieves me much for your sakes that the hand of the LORD is against me." Tears kept raining as Naomi described God as unjust and unkind in His punishment of them. Orpah had adored Naomi but could not defend Naomi's God. In that moment, Orpah determined her destiny. She kissed Naomi and tearfully agreed to go home to her parents. Ruth and Naomi watched, but Ruth made no move to follow. Naomi in astonishment asked, "Why are you standing here? Your sister-in-law has gone to her people and to her gods. Go. You must follow her."

Ruth shocked Naomi. "No! Entreat me not to leave you or to return from following you. Wherever you go, I am going. Wherever you lodge, I will lodge. Your people shall be my people. Your God is my God. Wherever you die, I will die, and there will I be buried. The LORD do so to me and more also if anything but death parts you and me." Ruth stood determined and would not release Naomi from her embrace until Naomi agreed.

At last Naomi sighed with relief and smiled, "You win, my daughter. I will speak no more of your leaving me." The two turned to the open road and began walking. They continued the journey until they crossed the

Ruth, an Unlikely Mother . . .

Jordan River and over the miles until they arrived in Bethlehem.

The entire little village welcomed Naomi in wonder at her alteration. "Is this really Naomi?" they asked. "Are you really Naomi?"

"Yes, of course, I am Naomi. But do not call me Naomi but rather call me Mara, for the Almighty has dealt very bitterly with me. I went out full from Bethlehem, but the LORD has brought me home again empty. Why then call me Naomi, seeing that the LORD has testified against me and has afflicted me?" The kindly villagers never referred to Naomi as Mara. She had been their pleasant friend and would always be remembered as one. Faith had taken Naomi home. Faith made Ruth decide to go with her. God turned tragedy to joy because of faith.

Grain crops were ripening when Naomi and Ruth arrived in town. "The barley harvest is beginning," Ruth noted. "I'll glean barley for us to have food." Naomi had no choice but to agree.

"I suppose you must, my daughter. All the fields look promising, but carefully choose so that you won't have to bounce from one field to another. I'll pray that the God of Israel will prosper your efforts and reward you for your kindness," Naomi kissed Ruth affectionately and waved good-bye.

Ruth chose a barley field and asked, "May I begin to glean after the reapers among the sheaves?" The foreman agreed and kept an eye on her all morning.

Later in the day, the owner of the field arrived to assess the harvesting. He entered the field with a familiar greeting, "The LORD be with you."

"The LORD bless you," the workers answered.

Boaz observed the bent body of a gleaner diligently working and inquired of the foreman, "Who is the young woman gleaning?"

The foreman chuckled, "She is the damsel from Moab who came back with Naomi. She asked to glean and to gather after the reapers among the sheaves. She has been working all day except for a short break in the house. She is totally focused upon her work."

"Thank you," Boaz said and strode to Ruth. "Hear me, my daughter. I am Boaz," he greeted. Ruth straightened her weary back and peered at the stranger, questioning such a presumptuous word, "daughter." Boaz continued, "Don't go to glean in another field. Don't leave my field, but stay close by my maidens. Keep your eyes on the field they reap, and follow them. I have given orders to the young men that they are not to touch you. When you get thirsty, help yourself to my drinking vessels. The young men keep them filled." He smiled at Ruth, noting her unassuming beauty and humility.

Ruth was so overwhelmed she fell on her face, bowing to the ground before Boaz. "Why have I found grace in your eyes? Who am I that you should notice me? I am a stranger," she blushed in amazement.

"I am fully aware of who you are. I've been informed of how you left your parents and your homeland and have come to live among a people you have never known. The LORD recompense your work. May you be given a full reward by the LORD God of Israel, under

Ruth, an Unlikely Mother . . .

whose wings you have come to trust."

"Thank you," Ruth replied. "Thank you for showing me favor and for comforting me. You have spoken most friendly to my heart, though I am not like one of your handmaidens." Ruth shyly smiled.

Boaz chuckled, "Oh, and at mealtime, you don't have to go home to eat. Just come to the lunch table and eat the food I have supplied for my workers." Ruth accepted the invitation, and at meal time she approached the lunch line with the reapers. She was warmly welcomed. Boaz was serving the food! "Here is parched corn for you," he said and gave her a generous helping. Ruth ate and returned to glean. Boaz noted her gracious manners and diligence to work. He gave orders to the young men working for him, "Let her glean among the sheaves, and do not scold her. Don't shame her or rebuke her. In fact, drop some handfuls along and leave them for her." Boaz left the field assured that Ruth would be safe and would gather enough to provide Naomi with plenty of grain.

Ruth gleaned until evening and beat the grain out of the husk. She returned home grateful for Boaz's generosity. Naomi was pleasantly surprised at the bushel of barley that Ruth had gleaned. She exclaimed, "Where have you gleaned today? In whose field did you work? Blessed be he that he did take notice."

"The man's name from whom I gleaned is Boaz," Ruth reported.

Naomi was ecstatic. Ruth did not understand the excitement, but she could appreciate the joy that Naomi

Nevertheless, God

expressed, "Bless him, LORD! You have not left off kindness to the living and to the dead." Turning to Ruth, she laughed, "Boaz is near of kin to us! Indeed, he is one of our closest kinsmen."

Ruth listened enthralled but not understanding the implications. She said, "He also said to me, 'You are to keep by my young men until they finish my harvest.'"

Naomi giggled knowingly, "It is good, my daughter, that you go out with Boaz's maidens so no one confronts you in any other field. You will be safe if you obey Boaz." Ruth was careful to please her mother-in-law and Boaz. She stayed near Boaz's workers until both the barley harvest and the wheat harvest were completed and the shocks of grain were neatly stacked in storage for threshing. She had returned each evening to Naomi with the day's gleanings.

Sheaves of barley were neatly stacked by Boaz's threshing floor to be threshed soon. Like most farmers, Boaz slept on his threshing floor to protect his harvest as he winnowed the grain to be stored in baskets and sacks.

Naomi knew the ritual and planned for Ruth's future. "Ruth, I shall seek for you a kinsman redeemer. Didn't I tell you that Boaz is our kinsman, the man with whose maidens you worked? Since the harvest is complete, Boaz will be winnowing barley in the threshing floor. He will work until he can't see; then he will sleep on the floor, guarding his grain.

"Listen carefully, and do as I say. We shall leave your future up to God and Boaz! You shall be as beautiful for Boaz as you were on the day my Mahlon claimed

Ruth, an Unlikely Mother . . .

you for his bride." Naomi chuckled and busied herself to hurry along her plans.

Ruth, as instructed, bathed, washed her hair, put on sweet perfume, and dressed in her widow's dress and the long, dark veil. Only her eyes were exposed in the evening shadows. Just before the city gate was closed, she slipped through, carefully avoiding people, and made her way to Boaz's threshing floor. She hid behind a large boulder and waited until she no longer could hear the thumping of threshing paddles beating the grain or smell the dusty husk being wafted away by the breeze as the grain was tossed gently into the air. The sound of falling grain had reminded her of a soft rain. In the glow of a small fire, she could see the man hunkered over the blaze. Every now and again he rotated a spit, skewering a lump of meat over the flame. The smell of roasting flesh tingled her nose. Soon he scooped the winnowed barley into a large basket and covered it. He then settled by the fire and ate.

She hid until she determined that Boaz had finished supper. His heart was merry, for he whistled a tune. She cautiously watched him make his bed. She peeked to see when he laid down and waited for the rhythmical purring of sleep. Padding softly across the boards, she crouched at his feet, then laid near to wait. She eased the cover off his feet as Naomi had instructed. Sleep eluded Ruth, for she did not know exactly what to expect should the man awaken. He snorted but slept on. Hours etched long shadows from a harvest moon across the night sky. A crier from the watchtower on the city wall called the night watch, "Midnight!"

The man started and bolted upright. Fear clouded his eyes. He stammered, "Woman, who are you?"

"I am Ruth, your handmaid," tumbled out the memorized words. "Spread therefore your skirt over me, for you are a near kinsman." Ruth was glad the darkness hid her burning embarrassment and shaking.

Boaz softened his voice, "Blessed are you of the LORD, my daughter. You have shown more kindness in this than you did in the beginning in that you have not pursued young men, poor or rich. But, my daughter, fear not. I will do all that you request. All my people know that you are a virtuous woman. It is true that I am near kin, but there is another man nearer of kin than I. You stay here until dawn, and in the morning, I will take care of the matter. As the LORD lives, I will. Go to sleep until the morning." Both laid down. With Ruth at his feet, Boaz pulled the cover over his toes and waited for dawn.

Tumultuous thoughts made sleep impossible for Ruth. *He must feel every emotion I feel. He is an older man than Mahlon. A woman my age usually longs to marry someone younger, but I cannot choose in my situation. He is right that I have not flirted with any young man. Whether he were rich or poor never entered my mind. All I have wanted was to provide food for Naomi and me. The dreams of a long marriage and a family were shattered when Mahlon died. Naomi's plan is now my only hope for a family.*

Before the rays of sun made visible the day, Boaz rolled out of his bed on the threshing floor. He spoke

Ruth, an Unlikely Mother . . .

kindly to Ruth, "Ruth, do not say a word about coming to my threshing floor. No one should hear that a woman spent the night here. Now, tie your veil around you like an apron, and hold it open like a pocket." Ruth did as he said. Boaz poured six measures of winnowed barley into the veil. Ruth tied the corners and slipped her hand under the knot. "Go, my daughter, before you will be seen," Boaz whispered.

Ruth bowed as graciously as her bundle allowed. "Thank you," she said. Tears threatened to spill down her bare cheeks.

Boaz watched her making her way toward the city gate, "I must be going her way soon to catch my kinsman as he comes out the gate to his fields." He smiled at the sound of the idea.

Ruth hurried home to Naomi. The older woman excitedly opened the door for her daughter-in-law. "Tell me," Naomi asked. "How was your adventure?"

"After we empty this pouch," Ruth said and took the bundle to the kitchen. She poured the barley into a large sack as Naomi held its mouth open.

"Now, tell me, who are you, my daughter?" she teased. She wiped her hands on her hips and returned to sit by the hearth, motioning for Ruth to sit beside her.

"Well, I did as you instructed, and Boaz woke up at midnight. He was frightened and surprised to see me, but he said that he would do all I required if he can."

"What do you mean, if he can?" Naomi inquired, her eyes big with questions.

"Boaz said that he is near of kin to us, but there is

another man nearer of kin than he. He said that today he will settle the matter with that other man. He gave me these six measures of barley to bring to you as a gift. I left before dawn."

Naomi clapped her hands and through tears of joy exulted, "Ruth, sit still, my daughter. Before this day is over, Boaz will finish his promise. Surely this very day you shall have a kinsman-redeemer husband!"

"You are so wise and clever, Mother! I can't ever thank you enough for loving me."

"Nonsense, my girl. It is I who cannot repay a debt so great to you," Naomi wiped damp, gray hair from her cheeks wet with tears. "You have been better to me than seven sons." The two women spent the morning eagerly waiting for a certain caller.

Boaz had left his threshing floor long before Ruth had finished telling Naomi her adventure in the barley field. He entered the narrow gate of Bethlehem before the wider gates had opened for the day. He positioned himself so he could see each individual coming to the gate. He set up an arrangement for seating several men and sat to wait and to watch. His fellow relative came briskly by the gate, intent on getting to work. "Ho, my brother!" Boaz called. He hurried to stop the man, "Turn aside and sit here. I have a legal situation that needs your immediate attention." The man obeyed. Boaz called ten elder men, who came to the gate. "Come, sit, and be witnesses for me in a legal matter that must be settled today," he requested. Before long the formalities began. Boaz announced, "Gentlemen, I have called upon you to

Ruth, an Unlikely Mother . . .

verify a transaction which must be made for the welfare of an elderly relative, Naomi. She has returned from Moab and wishes to sell our brother's land because he, Elimelech, is dead. There are only two left to redeem the property, my fellow kinsman and then me. It is my intent to advertise the sale to my kinsman in the presence of you witnesses." Turning to his relative, Boaz said, "Buy Elimelech's property now. If you won't, I will. You have first right to it. Will you redeem Naomi's property?"

"Of course I will!" the man beamed. "Elimelech's farm is a most desirable acquisition." He stirred, eager to get the process rolling.

Boaz cleared his throat and said, "You do know that the day you buy the land you must also buy it from Ruth, the Moabitess, the widow of Elimelech's son? You must know that the transaction requires that you marry Ruth and raise any children she has with you in the name of her dead husband. The property will always belong to those children."

The kinsman was bewildered. He thought Naomi was without any immediate family. If she were a totally dependent, old woman, he could provide her with a roof over her head for the few remaining years of life; then her property would become his forever. That would be wonderful. But the Moabite woman changed the picture entirely. He blanched and quenched his smile. He stammered, "I can't do that! Why, my own inheritance would be jeopardized. No. Boaz, on second thought, you redeem that property for yourself. I cannot."

Boaz reached and pulled off his kinsman's shoe.

Nevertheless, God

He held it high. "You ten elders are my witnesses that I have this day bought Elimelech's property from Naomi and that I declare Ruth to be my wife. This shoe is the signature for the legalities to be certified. I have today bought all that was Elimelech's, Chilion's, and Mahlon's from Naomi and from Ruth, Mahlon's widow. I have purchased Ruth to be my wife and to raise up the name of the dead upon his inheritance so that the name of Elimelech will not be cut off from among his kin. Are you in agreement as my witnesses?"

"We are witnesses," the elders shouted. "May the LORD make the woman you've taken as your wife to be like Rachel and like Leah, who did build the house of Israel. Boaz, do worthily in Ephratah, and be famous in Bethlehem. Let your house be like the house of Pharez, Judah's son by Tamar. The LORD give you children by this young woman. Amen!"

Boaz did not hesitate. He made quick strides to Naomi's door. Sweeping the two women into his muscular arms, he laughed and rejoiced with them in their good fortune. Boaz kissed his bride in a longing embrace of love. Ruth packed her few belongings and went with her husband. Several weeks passed before Ruth came with the announcement, "Naomi, you are now to become a grandmother. Boaz and I are having a baby!"

Naomi bubbled with joy. She could hardly wait to spread the news to friends. The months passed swiftly, and the baby was born. "You have a son, my daughter," Naomi kissed Ruth after having attended with the birth. She then went to inform Boaz.

Ruth, an Unlikely Mother . . .

The news spread quickly to friends. "Blessed be the LORD, which has not left you without a kinsman. May his name be famous in Israel. He shall be a restorer of your life and will nourish you in your old age. Your daughter-in-law, who loves you and has been better to you than seven sons, has given birth," they rejoiced.

Naomi took the child and held him close to her heart. She declared, "I shall gladly be your nurse, my grandson." He stopped crying and fell asleep.

"What shall be his name?" the women asked. The possibilities of names were suggested, and before the gaiety settled, the name Naomi approved was Obed.

Naomi became a doting grandmother, who told stories to the baby about ancestors, about his mother's courage, and about his father's kindness. The family tree was well leafed with those accountings of family history. The roots reached backward through hundreds of years to Abraham. The branches stretched upward through hundreds of years to Jesus Christ, the eternal Judge, who was born the descendant of Ruth and Boaz and their great-grandson, King David of Bethlehem.

EPILOGUE

Although the time of the judges did not actually end until Samuel had died long after he anointed Saul as king of Israel, Scripture does not chronicle the stories of the priest-judges, Eli and Samuel, among those of the Book of Judges. Their stories are recorded in the Book of I Samuel. Eli judged Israel for forty years, and Samuel judged for approximately sixty years, of which some years were simultaneous with the priesthood of Eli. Both those men left legacies of compromising sons, whose characters were not desirable as leaders. The citizens of Israel demanded a king to rule over them because they detested the behavior of those sons. Samuel continued to judge Israel even after he had anointed Saul and, later, David to be king. However, Samuel died several years before David actually ascended to the throne of Israel but not before he and David had ordained the proper Levites for particular offices in the service of the Tabernacle. Samuel and David wanted to assure that David's reign would begin with a proper relationship with God (I Chronicles 9:22).

Scripture continues the records of those tumultuous years of Israel's history through hundreds of years under various dynasties of kings, the civil war—which divided the country into two nations—their demise, and

Nevertheless, God

the rise from exile, united as one nation, Israel. However, there was no continuing story of any judges of Israel after Samuel's leadership ended. From that point on, her history focused on the stories of the kings and of the prophets sent from God to Israel.